MY BAHÁ'Í FAITH

a personal tour of the Bahá'í teachings

By Justice St Rain

SPECIAL IDEAS

My Bahá'í Faith
A Personal Tour of the Bahá'í Teachings
Copyright © 2003 by Justice St Rain

OTHER BOOKS BY THIS AUTHOR:

Falling Into Grace
The Trials and Triumphs of Becoming a Bahá'í

Why Me?
A Spiritual Guide to Growing Through Tests

Poor in All Save God
A Spiritual Guide to Wealth

All quotations are from the Sacred Writings of the Bahá'í
Faith unless otherwise noted, © National Spiritual Assembly of the United States, used by permission.
Cover design by Justice St Rain.

Special Ideas
PO Box 9, Heltonville, IN 47436
1-800-326-1197
www.special-ideas.com

ISBN# 1-888547-15-4

Printed in the USA
10 9 8 7 6 5 4 3 2 1
04 05 06 07 08 09 10 11 12 13 14

MY BAHÁ'Í FAITH

a personal tour of the bahá'í teachings

The Bahá'í Faith is a wonderful religion. It has been my religion of choice since I decided to join it at the age of seventeen. Since you are apparently curious, I would like to tell you a little bit about what it teaches, how it started, and why I decided to adopt it as my personal path of growth.

Like many people who grew up in this country, I was raised Christian. I attended Sunday school as a child and sat with my mother through countless church services from the time I was old enough to sit still until I reached the edge of adulthood. I was the youngest confirmed member of my church at 12, took Communion, and served as an acolyte for a year. I loved Jesus, I loved the principles of peacefulness and kindness that He taught, and it made me feel good to know that I was aligned with all that was good and right.

But somewhere in junior high, I began to struggle with the whole question of Salvation. Salvation sounded like a fine thing when I was young and everyone I knew was also saved. But as I matured and began to look beyond the confines of my small world, I became uncomfortable with the thought that my new Jewish friends might somehow be deserving of the wrath of God in spite of their obvious kindness and friendliness. I listened to the song "My Sweet Lord" by the ex-Beatle George Harrison and realized that Christianity was not the only religion in the world. In fact, there were more non-Christians in the world than Christians. This meant that according to my existing beliefs, the majority of the world was damned to hell. This perspective no longer made sense to me. It felt fundamentally wrong.

My faith in the underlying virtues of love, compassion, forgiveness and humility was stronger than my faith in the creeds that I had worked so hard to memorize. I believed that God was bigger than the petty retribution that was being attributed to Him, and so I left the church and started looking for a new understanding of my relationship with the unknown and the infinite.

According to my original beliefs, the majority of the world was damned to hell.

I must admit that this was over thirty years ago. You might say that many churches are no longer focusing on hellfire, damnation, and blood sacrifice, and you would be right. But just because it is less of a focus does not mean that it is not still at the very core of most Christian theology. The promise of Salvation requires, by definition, that we be saved *from something.* My understanding of Christianity was that we were being saved from some form of punishment. Since I could not imagine a loving God doing *anything* hurtful or unkind to anyone simply because he or she did not believe in something, I felt I had to reject this core tenet of Christian beliefs.

The next few years of my life were spent on a dual path. On one hand, I pursued all the normal distractions of a young teen—exploring drugs, alcohol, romance, and rebellion. On the other hand, I took an unusual interest in alternative spiritual disciplines. I practiced meditation, and yoga, went to Bible study classes to challenge the teachers, and read about philosophy, psychology, Buddhism, Hinduism, metaphysics and parapsychology. What I was looking for was a system of belief that was both logical and loving, a way to feel connected with something both transcendent and kind.

Here is the crux of my dilemma: Once I had decided that the concept of salvation was not consistent with my vision of a loving God, I was left with what appeared to be two equally unacceptable options. I could either abandon religion entirely, which would leave me with no source of guidance on my path towards God, or I could choose from one of the remaining major religions. But the very fact that there were so many religions to choose from was itself disturbing. They all offered many teachings that were the same and seemed to come from God, yet they each also had teachings that were different. And of course most of them claimed, like Christianity, to be the only path to God. It was as though God were in competition with Himself. I was tempted to agree with the philosopher Voltaire who said that the differences between religions proved that they were all false. But then wouldn't their similarities prove that they were all true? How could I reconcile this dilemma?

In 1972, the Bahá'í Faith was still a relatively unknown religion in the United States, so it was a "miracle" you might say, that there was a Bahá'í student in my high school biology class. We were both considered strange by our peers, so we quickly became friends. He was somewhat amused by my attempts at creating my own religion from scratch by combining the best of everything I found elsewhere. He told me about Bahá'u'lláh, the Prophet-Founder of the Bahá'i Faith, and tried to explain to me what Bahá'ís call "the three onenesses"—one loving God, one unfolding religion, and one human family. I was intrigued by many of the teachings, but at sixteen I was in love with my own brilliance and was not ready to join someone else's religion, no matter how reasonable.

My friend moved away, and I spent a year forgetting everything he had told me. Or I thought I had. When a second friend "discovered" the Bahá'í teachings, I realized that I had slowly internalized much of what I had heard before. I was finally able to admit that the teachings of Bahá'u'lláh really did resolve my two dilemmas concerning salvation and the common foundation of religion.

✳ **MY BAHÁ'Í FAITH**

AN ALTERNATE
VIEW OF SALVATION:

The Bahá'í Teachings resolved my discomfort with the concept of salvation by offering completely new responses to four simple questions.

What am I being saved from?
Why do I need to be saved?
Why can't I save myself?
What do I have to do to be saved?

What am I being saved from?

Like Christ, Bahá'u'lláh teaches that God wants to save me—but *not* from some outside force (the devil) or some external punishment (hell), and not even from my own supposedly innate sinfulness. God's great desire for me is to save me from my complete and utter ignorance of my own true self.

God's goal is to help me redefine *who* I am, *why* I was created, and *how* I can achieve my fullest potential. God wants me to learn, grow, love and be happy.

If we see a plant that does not grow, we call it dead. Likewise a human soul that does not grow and learn and become what God meant for it to be is *spiritually* dead. There is no worse "punishment" than this. Bahá'u'lláh says, *"True loss is for him whose days have been spent in utter ignorance of his self."*

We are all born ignorant, but with an immense capacity to learn and grow.

Why Do I Need to Be Saved?

The usual answer to this question is that we are sinful—that because of original sin we deserve punishment and are unworthy of God's grace. But if we replace the word "sinful" with the word "ignorant," then we can easily recognize our innate need

4

for education without feeling any shame for not being perfect to begin with. We are all born ignorant, but with an immense capacity to learn and grow. We are born not knowing who we really are, and not having lived up to our full potential. This is obvious.

Why do I need help to be saved?

What is not so obvious is why we are in need of Jesus—or any other Prophet—as an outside source of guidance. Why can't we "save ourselves?" That is, why can't we figure out who we are on our own? Plants don't need teachers in order to grow and blossom, why do we?

We need God to send us these Divine Educators for the simple fact that people learn primarily through example. We study and observe the people and things around us and come to conclusions about how things work and how we should behave. If humans were simply animals, then we could learn everything we need to know by observing other animals. But we aren't. Humans have souls. We are infused with the Holy Spirit. Our souls operate under a different set of laws and are guided by a different set of principles than animal instinct. In order to learn how to behave like humans, we need spiritual examples. This spiritual example *has to* come from outside the normal worldly plane.

If people followed the example of animals, we would live by the "law of the jungle," but God wants us to follow the Golden Rule. When we explore the example of the *physical* world, we find that it is limited and prone to chaos. When we explore our *spiritual* reality, we find that we are unlimited, creative and full of love. This does not mean that the material world is *evil*. It simply means that the material world is an inadequate example for us to follow when we are trying to explore our uniquely human potential.

With all of the examples of limited physical reality that surround us, it is *essential* that God save us from a material perspective by providing us with spiritual examples. We cannot create these examples or discover these truths on our own. That is why God sent us Jesus Christ. That is how He saved us. The example of the life and teachings of Jesus Christ *save us* from the degradation of a purely material, animal existence. That is how *all* of God's spiritual Teachers save us from ignorance of our true spiritual selves.

With all of the examples of limited physical reality that surround us, it is **essential** *that God save us from a material perspective by providing us with spiritual examples.*

Because these Messengers have been providing positive examples since the beginning of time, we might try to convince ourselves that we don't really need them. But if we try to imagine a world in which there never were any spiritual examples, it becomes clear that we would not have "discovered" the Golden Rule (let alone "turn the other cheek") by observing nature alone.

What do I have to do to be saved?

The two competing answers to this question that we hear from most Christians is that we are either saved by faith or saved by works. Bahá'ís say that both are required. First, I have to have faith that God knows more about me than I know about myself. Second, I have to be able to recognize, believe in and love God's Teachers when He sends them. This is no small task. But salvation is not a one-time event. It is a process of discovery and growth. So in addition to these initial acts of faith, salvation also requires a lifetime of effort, action and strength of will on my part to live up to my full capacity.

Becoming my true self

Becoming my true self involves loving God and obeying God. It involves loving God's virtues, and *living* those virtues in my daily life.

Bahá'u'lláh explains that we are all created in the "image of God." We "reflect" God when we develop our God-given virtues such as love, compassion, honesty, reverence and courage. He says:

O SON OF MAN! Veiled in My immemorial being and in the ancient eternity of My essence, I knew My love for thee; therefore I created thee, have engraved on thee Mine image and revealed to thee My beauty.   — *Bahá'u'lláh*

Loving, learning, growing, living, reflecting virtues, being human, being obedient—these are not separate processes. They are different ways of looking at the same thing. When we embrace the process, then we are assured of eternal life and growth. And when we resist the process, we begin to wither and die.

This simple explanation of what God was saving me from, why and how, made a lot of sense to me. I suddenly understood so much more of what Jesus had been saying. There was no longer a conflict between the idea of salvation and my faith in God's loving-kindness.

The relationship between religions

As soon as I understood the nature of salvation, my second dilemma concerning the relationship between the world's religions became clear as well. I realized the simple truth that all major religions come from the same source. Some of you will have already noticed that I use Bahá'u'lláh's name and Jesus' name in the same sentence as though they were equal. There is a reason for that.

If the purpose of life is to get to heaven and avoid hell, and if God requires a blood sacrifice to allow that to happen, then Jesus is a one-time-only-sacrificial-lamb, and belief in Him is your sole ticket to heaven. But if salvation is a path of discovery; a process of education; then it would make sense for God to send us more than one teacher, and reach out to people in more than one time and place.

God loves *everyone.* Let me say that again: God loves *everyone*—and *everyone* is in need of education and guidance. Think about that. God loves the Chinese, the African, the people living today and the people living 5,000 years ago. A loving parent wouldn't send one child to school and leave the rest to grow up wild in the woods! God is a much wiser parent than we are. *Of course* God has found a way to guide humanity throughout history and around the world.

one God, one teacher, many names

Because there is only one God, every Divine Teacher represents that same God and speaks on His behalf. Think of it this way: you and I have both had many teachers in school. On one hand, each was a unique individual who taught us the specific things that we needed to understand at that point in time. From another perspective, all of those teachers could be understood as one teacher—each one building on the lessons of the one who came before. If our parents told us that in order to learn we had to listen to our teacher, we didn't assume that they were only talking about one teacher, but all teachers. Likewise, if an individual teacher said, "Listen to me! If you don't listen to me, then you won't learn anything," she didn't mean that you shouldn't listen to your teacher next year, or that you should forget what you were taught the year before.

> *Because there is only one God, every Divine Teacher represents that same God*

When Christ said, "I am the Way, the Truth and the Life. No man cometh to the Father except by Me," He was speaking as one of God's chosen teachers. There is no way to be "saved," that is, to become the person God wants us to become, unless we follow the guidance and example of His teachers. The Founders of the world's great religions are all teachers of God. Abraham, Moses, Krishna, Christ, Buddha, Mohammed, and Bahá'u'lláh all lived lives that were shining examples. They all spoke with the same God-given authority. Their goal was to teach us about ourselves and about how to grow closer to God by developing our virtues.

so why do these teachers look and sound so different?

The idea that all religions come from God and all of the Founders of these religions are equal is certainly a challenging one. It deserves serious thought and prayer. It also requires two more key concepts in order to make complete sense: Progress and Diversity.

Of the major religions still active on earth today, Zoroastrianism, Judaism, Christianity and Islam all trace their roots back to Abraham. So why are they so different? Consider this: The reason why your high school teacher taught you different material *and* taught using a different style than your elementary school teacher is *not* because your high school teacher was necessarily any smarter than your earlier teachers. It was because *you* were more mature and had a greater understanding of the world. Your needs and your capacity both changed. We call that maturity when we are talking about individuals. We call it *progress* when we talk about civilization as a whole. Bahá'u'lláh explained something that we call *progressive revelation*. It is the simple idea that God reveals ideas, information and guidance in a progressive order, based on our changing needs and our capacity to understand.

Alongside progress, there is the beauty of diversity. Buddhism and Hinduism reflect the personalities of cultures that are very different from those of the West. Since human virtues are infinite, there are many paths that can help us uncover our vast potential. Once we let go of the idea that there is only *one way* to be saved, we can see that there must be *many ways* to learn and grow. God has given the world many different and equally valid examples of spiritual growth.

Within the context of both progress and diversity, religion offers us guidance in two different categories: spiritual and material. Because God loves us, He wants us to grow spiritually and survive physically. Each religion, therefore, offers two very different sets of teachings.

The Golden Rule is a good example of a spiritual teaching. The Golden Rule is a good example of a spiritual teaching. Spiritual teachings are common to all of the world's religions. They speak of love, humility, generosity, honesty, service to others, and detachment from material pleasures. They are the teachings that help us discover who we are, why we are here, and how we grow towards God. Though these teachings are universal, each Prophet has explained them in the language and style that were appropriate for the people of Their time and place. Virtues such as obedience, sacrifice and faith, for example, are understood very differently at different stages of maturity. Virtues such as humility, peacefulness and detachment are understood differently between different cultures.

The material teachings, sometimes referred to as the *social* teachings, are unique to each religion and are specifically revealed to meet the physical needs of a particular time, place and culture. They tell us how to organize families, clans, tribes or nations, and how to avoid unhealthy foods and behaviors. They offer stories that inspire spiritual growth and provide punishments that motivate appropriate behavior. These teachings make perfect sense when viewed from an historical perspective, but when they clash with a modern, multi-cultural world, they can cause disunity and confusion. Understanding the original purpose of social teachings allows us to adjust them to current needs without feeling that we are betraying God.

Personally, being able to look at all of the world's religions and see them not as competitors, but as cooperative chapters in a single book of revelation, lifted a giant weight off my shoulders. Viewing them in a cultural and historical perspective, I could recognize the good in all, while judging and damning none. I could see God's universal wisdom in the similarities, and His infinite kindness in the differences.

Somewhere along the way I experienced a kind of "ah-hah!" moment—a Pentecostal awakening you might say—in which everything finally made sense.

Somewhere along the way I experienced a kind of "ah-*hah*!" moment—a Pentecostal awakening you might say—in which everything finally made sense. I made a leap of faith, but not of *blind* faith. It was a deep, abiding certainty that everything fit together and formed a secure and rational foundation that could support an eternity of spiritual growth. It was *conscious knowledge,* as the Bahá'í Writings say, that God's love for me, my love for God, my spiritual growth, the progress of human kind, the station of Christ, the teachings of Moses, the spirituality of Buddha, the entire history of religion and the entire destiny of the human race all fit into a beautiful, organic, evolving web of life that left no one out and welcomed every soul's participation.

From that moment on, I was a Bahá'í. Thirty years of ups and downs, challenges and rewards, friendships and frustrations have not dimmed that initial flash of insight. I could no more deny its truth than I could deny gravity. And like gravity, it has kept my spiritual foundation anchored in reality.

So here is the foundation I finally came to believe in after my four years of searching:

That God loves everyone.
That the purpose of my life is to love God in return.
That I love God by reflecting His virtues.
That I am not deserving of punishment,
*   but in need of guidance.*
That Guidance is available in all of the
*   world's religions.*
That Bahá'u'lláh is the most recent source of
*   that guidance.*

The foundation I started with over thirty years ago continues to help me make sense of both the Bahá'í teachings and the teachings of every other religion I come in contact with. Of course, it is *only* a foundation. The Bahá'í Writings that build on these core teachings would fill a small library. There are many detailed explanations of our relationship to God, the role and station of the Prophets of God, their relationship to one another, the nature of our soul, the path towards virtue, and the social tools that will help us progress as a civilization. So if this foundation makes even a little bit of sense to you; if you have caught even a glimmer of an "ah-*hah*!" out of the corner of your mind, then I encourage you to keep reading as I tell you about some of the other Bahá'í teachings that I fell in love with when I became a Bahá'í.

MY DISCLAIMER

Before I start, however, I would like to protect you and me both with the ultimate disclaimer. There is no one alive on earth who can tell you what the Bahá'í teachings mean or what the Bahá'í community will ultimately look like. All any of us can do is offer our opinions and observations based on our reading of the Bahá'í Sacred Writings.

All any of us can do is offer our opinions and observations .

Bahá'u'lláh quoted an Islamic tradition that says: *"We speak one word, and by it we intend one and seventy meanings; each one of these meanings we can explain."* In other words, every word of revelation has 71 different possible meanings. This means, that the six-word phrase "I knew My love for thee," for example, would have over a hundred billion possible combinations of meanings. That's a lot more possible meanings than there are people on earth. What this means *to me* is that each of us must decide what Bahá'u'lláh wants us to get out of His words. It also means that Bahá'ís have to learn to agree to disagree—even on points of theology and principle that are very near and dear to their hearts— in order to maintain the central principle of unity in diversity.

This does not mean that the Bahá'í Community is in a constant state of tension—quite the contrary, it is very loving and unified. What it does mean is that we are often in a state of flux, as different perspectives become popular for a while and then fade. I know Bahá'ís who look at the Bahá'í Writings through a "new age" lens, and talk about astrology and Rumi. Other Bahá'ís are very pragmatic, redefining Bahá'í teachings in scientific terms. There are Bahá'ís who were born-again Christians looking for the return of the Spirit of Christ, and others who were atheists. Some take every word of the Writings literally and could tell you *exactly* how many different meanings there are in a six-word sentence (128,100,283,921), while others are content to know that there are more than two meanings, (at least one of which is not

literal). The amazing thing is that instead of arguing and splitting into six (or six thousand) different denominations as other religions have, they remain united around their love for God, their recognition of Bahá'u'lláh, and their quest for spiritual growth, using the Bahá'í principles as their guide.

Many introductory Bahá'í books are written in the third person, as though the author represented some "official" Bahá'í perspective. In order to avoid controversy, they have to stick with the most common explanations and the most basic principles. I've chosen to admit from the beginning that these are only my opinions. This allows me to offer insights and ideas that I feel very strongly about, but about which other Bahá'ís might disagree. That's why I've entitled this book *MY Bahá'í Faith*—so you will feel comfortable discovering a different Bahá'í Faith of your own.

> *I've entitled this book* **MY Bahá'í Faith** *—so you will feel comfortable discovering a different Bahá'í Faith of your own.*

a word about the language of revelation

Throughout this book, I will be sharing with you quite a few of my favorite quotations from the Bahá'í Writings. Unless you spend your spare time reading the King James Bible and the poetry of Rumi, Kahil Gibran, and Shakespeare, you will probably find the language beautiful, but somewhat difficult to follow at times. You may be tempted to say, "Why doesn't He just come out and say what He means?!" Well, for a lot of reasons, some of which I will try to explain now.

Bahá'u'lláh wrote in Persian and Arabic. When His words were translated into English, the translators tried to capture the elegance, reverence and poetry of the original. If you enjoy poetry, you know that a few words of poetry can express more about the human condition and the longings of the heart than many volumes of technical prose. There is no way for Bahá'u'lláh to condense "seventy-one meanings" into each word if those words are not arranged in rich, complex and meaningful ways that utilize symbol, simile, analogy, parable and metaphor.

A few words of poetry can express more about the human condition and the longings of the heart than many volumes of technical prose.

Our ability to both recognize and understand these literary tools is critical to our ability to intellectually understand spiritual reality.

Metaphor is a figure of speech in which one thing is spoken of as if it were another. For example, the Bahá'í writings use the phrase "the Sun of Reality," to refer to God.

Simile is like a metaphor except that it acknowledges the fact that the two things are not *really* identical things by using the word *like*. For example, God is like the sun.

A metaphor implies an analogy, while a simile invites you to look for the analogy. An analogy is when you say that because two things have one thing in common, they may have other things in common as well. This means that you can learn more about the second thing by studying the first. So, for example, if I call God the Sun of Reality, I am implying that if you think about the qualities of the sun, you will come to understand more about God.

Parable is essentially an extended metaphor told in story form.

A symbol is different from these things, in that there is not necessarily any relationship between the qualities of a symbol and the qualities of the thing it represents. For example, ♥ is a symbol for the human heart, even though the shape bears little resemblance to the physical organ. The human heart, however, can be used as a metaphor, simile or analogy for our emotional center because they are both essential for our survival, and may have other qualities in common.

Trying to explain spiritual truths without the use of any metaphor at all is virtually impossible.

So why am I giving you this little review of literary terms? Because trying to explain spiritual truths without the use of any metaphor *at all* is virtually impossible. There is really only one word in the English language that accurately describes the soul, and that is "ineffable." It means "beyond words" or "too sacred to be spoken." The words we try to use, like *grow, progress, move, closer, farther, reflect,* or *illumine* are all, themselves, only weak metaphors for whatever it is that the soul actually does. And, as I said, the physical world is not an adequate mirror for the human soul. So these limited, material words have to be combined in a way that elevates their meaning.

Bahá'u'lláh's son, 'Abdu'l-Bahá, explained that:

Divine things are too deep to be expressed by common words. The heavenly teachings are expressed in parable in order to be understood and preserved for ages to come. When the spiritually minded dive deeply into the ocean of their meaning they bring to the surface the pearls of their inner significance. There is no greater pleasure than to study God's Word with a spiritual mind.

The object of God's teaching to man is that man may know himself in order to comprehend the greatness of God.

This quotation itself is a good example of the use of metaphor to express deeper meaning. To "dive deeply into the ocean of their meaning" means the same as to "work hard to understand," but it evokes a much more satisfying image that stimulates the imagination. Your heart, mind, and even your body can have a visceral response to the mental image of a deep-sea plunge. So when he says "There is no greater pleasure," it rings truer than it would have after the phrase "work hard." Personally, I derive great pleasure from "diving into" these words again and again—sinking down into the watery world of possibility only to emerge, breathless, to the surface of my understanding with a radiant new pearl of wisdom clutched in my hands. See, doesn't that sound like fun?

People's inability to recognize a metaphor for what it is has caused a great deal of confusion and disunity.

In the past, people's inability to recognize a metaphor for what it is has caused a great deal of confusion, disunity and even wars within and between religions. For example, the literal reading of the metaphor of Father and Son has caused a thousand years of conflict between Christians and Moslems.

While the ability to recognize metaphor, simile and analogy are essential for our ability to intellectually *understand* spiritual reality, it is *not* required for actually *being* spiritual. Being spiritual is the result of recognizing, loving and practicing *virtues*. Fortunately, even a child can do that. Indeed, even a mentally handicapped quadriplegic can recognize, feel and return the essential virtue of love. I believe that this is why Bahá'u'lláh said *"...that every man hath been, and will continue to be, able of*

himself to appreciate the Beauty of God, the Glorified." As long as we stay focused on the beauty of God, we can enjoy the pleasure of exploring hidden meanings without feeling tempted to fight over our different interpretations.

Anyway, the point is that the pleasure of studying God's word *"with a spiritual mind"* is worth the extra effort it takes to read the lofty language of revelation. Instead of thinking to yourself, "look at all of those big, flowery words," take a moment to reflect on the meanings behind the images.

In order to maintain the flow of the book, I have limited each section to just a couple of relevant quotations. There is a bibliography in the back when you are ready to explore these topics more deeply.

The other thing you need to know about the language of these writings is that the English language does not have a gender-neutral pronoun that is appropriate for referring to God. Arabic does, but when translating into English, the translators have chosen to use the masculine "He." God, of course, is neither male nor female, but is spirit. Please forgive the limits of the language, and feel free to substitute a feminine pronoun in your head as you read these writings.

One last piece of housekeeping before we "dive" into the body of the book: I will be using a lot of quotations from the writings of both Bahá'u'lláh and 'Abdu'l-Bahá. I will tell you a lot about both of Them in the section on history, but for now, all you need to know is that Bahá'u'lláh is the Prophet-Founder of the Bahá'í Faith, and 'Abdu'l-Bahá is His son and authorized interpreter.

THE PATH OF SPIRITUAL GROWTH

THE DAY IN WHICH WE LIVE

The concept of progressive revelation that I discussed briefly before, is based on the premise that the human race as a whole is maturing along a path similar to that of an individual. To me, next to the realization that God loves everyone, this is the most exciting idea in the Bahá'í teachings. It explains so much, answers so many questions, and gives me so much hope for the future that I sometimes wonder how I could face the world without it.

The human race as a whole is maturing along a path similar to that of an individual.

If you have ever studied child development, or if you have raised a child yourself, you probably already know that children go through a series of distinct developmental stages. It is not just that children learn more as they grow. As they mature, the way in which they *think* changes dramatically. This is particularly true when a child reaches adolescence. Four different capacities develop around that time. First is the shift from concrete, literal thinking to the ability to reason in the abstract. Our ability to recognize and understand metaphor increases with maturity and takes a giant leap forward at adolescence. This is when teens become able to wrestle with the concept of God, infinity, free will, etc. Before this time, the words are there, but the understanding of them is firmly grounded in the material side of the metaphor. As I explained earlier, this shift is critical to our ability to understand spiritual teachings.

Second, teens acquire the ability to reason morally based on principles, not just rules. Things are no longer right or wrong based on memorized rules of conduct or the fear of punishment. The concepts of good and bad lose their black and white crispness, and become better or worse.

As we mature, we develop abstract reasoning, moral reasoning, personal responsibility and increased material capabilities.

Third, a sense of personal responsibility develops. What we call the "locus of control" moves inward. Choices are made based on what *they* think and feel, not what parents or teachers have said.

Finally, alongside all of these new inner powers comes the physical strength and development to act on them.

The result of these four new powers is a period of intense confusion, identity crisis, rebellion and self-discovery, followed by the eventual emergence of an independent, mature, stable, responsible and capable adult.

Yes, there are some adults who never get over adolescence, and some adolescents who self-destruct before they become adults. But the vast majority of people who enter the period of adolescence eventually arrive on the other side as adults.

Having said that, it is also evident that, even though they are capable of abstract, moral, internally directed thinking, many adults live a large percentage of their lives in the black and white, "concrete operational," externally directed world of their childhoods. Just as there were people in Jesus' time who wanted to know how they could crawl back into the womb to be "born again," there are many adults today who are looking for physical evidence of a metaphoric reality. True maturity is not measured by what we are capable of, but how we actually live our lives.

Likewise, we could say that the maturity of civilization *as a whole* is not based on the capacity of its brightest and most mature members, but is, rather, some kind of average based on how people actually act as groups.

Bahá'u'lláh explains that humans, as a group, are caught up in a period of confusion, chaos and rebellion similar to adolescence, and that we are on the cusp of maturity.

This understanding helps explain four things. First, it gives us another clue as to why religions of the past took different approaches to teaching us about God. The older a religion is, the more physical its description of God, the more black & white its laws, and the harsher its external sources of punishment. This is not because the Prophets of these religions were less mature. It is because They shaped Their messages to match the capacity of Their followers.

Second, it helps explain why the world is in such chaos. As we mature we become disillusioned with the systems and controls we have lived with for centuries. We flex our technological muscles and discover power we never dreamed we would have. Conflicts develop between those who still view the world in concrete, black & white terms and those who are ready to explore a more flexible world view.

Third, it gives us hope for the future. Adolescence is a good thing, in spite of its difficulty, because without it we cannot become adults. It is also a temporary condition that has a predictable outcome. No matter what happens in the short term, we can predict with confidence that the civilization of the future will be more mature. This means, among other things, that it will be more peaceful, more just, more organized, more productive. It will allow for abstract thought, principle-based laws and morals, personal freedoms and responsibilities, and a broad appreciation of diversity. This is why Bahá'ís everywhere are looking towards the future with great optimism and confidence.

DEVELOPING A MATURE
RELATIONSHIP WITH GOD

*Who can doubt that such a consummation—the coming of age
of the human race—must signalize, in its turn, the inauguration of
a world civilization such as no mortal eye hath ever beheld or human
mind conceived? Who is it that can imagine the lofty standard which
such a civilization, as it unfolds itself, is destined to attain? Who can
measure the heights to which human intelligence, liberated from its
shackles, will soar? Who can visualize the realms which the human
spirit, vitalized by the outpouring light of Bahá'u'lláh, shining in the
plenitude of its glory, will discover?*   — Shoghi Effendi*

There is one final insight that the concept of a maturing
humanity has to offer. This is the realization that, as the most
recent of the world's religions, the Bahá'í Faith is specifically
designed to meet the needs of a mature human race. More
importantly, it is God's way of inviting us, individually and col-
lectively, into a deeper, more loving, more *mature* relationship
with Him.

Just as a parent must wait many years to have an adult relationship with his or her child, God has waited thousands of years
to have a relationship with a mature human race. There are
many things God has wanted to tell us, but we could not bear to
hear them.

Now we can. Now *you* can.

This deeper and more mature relationship is possible because a mature humanity is better able to interpret and understand abstract ideas when presented in metaphor, symbol and
allegory. We are better able to look beyond the literal interpretation to figure out the practical application of God's message.
Because of this, Bahá'u'lláh is able to use deeper, richer, more
complex, profound and intimate symbols and metaphors when
describing His relationship with us.

GOÒ'S LOVE FOR US

As the Bahá'í writings say, *"...the core of religious faith is that mystical feeling which unites man with God."* Humanity has not yet begun to explore the implications of a loving and mature friendship with God. This is not to suggest that we have somehow become equals with God. God, as I will discuss soon, is beyond our ability to comprehend. What it *does* suggest is that we can seek the unapproachable as adults rather than as children, fully engaged rather than in a state of fear or shame. We can explore a mature relationship between unequals. This allows for a completely new kind of interaction. What would that look like? How would it feel? How might God describe it? Where would it lead?

While 'Abdu'l-Bahá often uses Jesus' Father/child metaphor when talking about our relationship with God, Bahá'u'lláh describes our relationship with God in more intimate and mature language. Speaking as the Mouthpiece of God Himself, Bahá'u'lláh extends the following invitation:

> *For whereas in days past every lover besought and searched after his Beloved, it is the Beloved Himself Who now is calling His lovers and is inviting them to attain His presence.* — *Bahá'u'lláh*

> *O SON OF THE WONDROUS VISION! I have breathed within thee a breath of My own Spirit, that thou mayest be My lover. Why hast thou forsaken Me and sought a beloved other than Me?*
> — *Bahá'u'lláh*

When God says He wants us to become His "lover," He is trusting a mature mind to look beyond the literal interpretation and explore the metaphor's many useful insights. Attraction, longing, passion, faithfulness, intimacy, honesty, abandon, intensity, joy—these are all appropriate virtues to apply to our relationship with God—virtues that we might not apply to a more fatherly image of God.

Bahá'u'lláh uses other metaphors as well that are, perhaps, less romantic, but certainly no less intimate. He speaks of knowing us, loving us, engraving His image on us, living within us, and breathing life into us, and He invites us to respond appropriately.

O SON OF MAN! Veiled in My immemorial being and in the ancient eternity of My essence, I knew My love for thee; therefore I created thee, have engraved on thee Mine image and revealed to thee My beauty. — *Bahá'u'lláh*

O SON OF MAN! I loved thy creation, hence I created thee. Wherefore, do thou love Me, that I may name thy name and fill thy soul with the spirit of life. — *Bahá'u'lláh*

O SON OF DUST! All that is in heaven and earth I have ordained for thee, except the human heart, which I have made the habitation of My beauty and glory; yet thou didst give My home and dwelling to another than Me;.... — *Bahá'u'lláh*

a mature love for god

So what is the appropriate human response to God's love? How does one take these beautiful metaphors and transform them into practical behavior? It seems to me that this is the central question of religion. If we get this answer wrong, then not much else really matters. And yet, it appears to be a very difficult question.

The limitations of human language are never more clear than when we try to express what it means to love and be loved by an Infinite, Unknowable, All-Powerful Intangible Divine Essence. It doesn't really matter if you use the words Lover, Father, or Friend. They are all inadequate. One thing that they all have in common, however, is that they imply an intimacy, a process of coming closer, becoming nearer to God. I find 'Abdu'l-Bahá's description of this process very helpful.

Therefore, we learn that nearness to God is possible through devotion to Him, through entrance into the Kingdom and service to humanity; it is attained by unity with mankind and through loving-kindness to all; it is dependent upon investigation of truth, acquisition of praiseworthy virtues, service in the cause of universal peace and personal sanctification. In a word, nearness to God necessitates sacrifice of self, severance and the giving up of all to Him. Nearness is likeness. — 'Abdu'l-Bahá

To reflect God, to be engraved with His image, to be *like* God is to be near Him, and to be near Him is to acquire His virtues and apply them in service to humanity.

Here is an excellent summary:

In a word, the "image and likeness of God" constitute the virtues of God, and man is intended to become the recipient of the effulgences of divine attributes. This is the essential foundation of all the divine religions, the reality itself, common to all.

— 'Abdu'l-Bahá

In these two sentences, 'Abdu'l-Bahá translates the critical elements of all of scripture's lofty metaphors, symbols and parables, and condenses them into one word: Virtues. He then proclaims that *the essential foundation* of all religion is God's desire for us to acquire these virtues.

God loved us by engraving our souls **We love God when we** with His image—which means He gave **love His virtues.** us His own virtues. This is the practical explanation of the "God's love for us" side of the equation. So what is the practical version of our response?

We love God when we love His virtues.

We *demonstrate* our love for Him by becoming more like God—that is, by practicing His virtues.

Virtues are God's gift of love to us. Virtues are our gift of loving gratitude in return.

Put another way, it is impossible to love God without loving His virtues, and it is impossible to love His virtues without bringing them out in ourselves.

So it seems that by applying a mature, intelligent analysis to God's profound and mystical expressions of love for us, we have discovered a simple, practical approach to loving God in return—an approach so simple that even a child can understand it.

We love God by loving the virtues of God that are reflected within ourselves and within the people around us.

Here are a few more quotations that support the role of virtues in deepening our relationship with God.

> *The good pleasure of God is love for His creatures. The will and plan of God is that each individual member of humankind shall become illumined like unto a lamp, radiant with all the destined virtues of humanity, leading his fellow creatures out of natural darkness into the heavenly light.* 'Abdu'l-Bahá

> *Therefore, you must thank God that He has bestowed upon you the blessing of life and existence in the human kingdom. Strive diligently to acquire virtues befitting your degree and station. Be as lights of the world which cannot be hid and which have no setting in horizons of darkness.* 'Abdu'l-Bahá

> *'What is the purpose of our lives?'*
> *'Abdu'l-Baha. - 'To acquire virtues.'*

The idea that God loves us by giving us virtues, we love God by loving His virtues, and we demonstrate our love by practicing our virtues may seem rather circular, but it is simply elegant. It is also not as simple as it sounds. God's virtues are infinite. No matter how hard we work, or how long we try, we will never perfect all of them. In order to receive them, we have to learn to love them. In order to love them, we have to learn how to recognize them. In order to recognize them, we have to learn how to perceive them using our spiritual perceptions. This is where exploring God's teachings, engaging in service, exercising our free will, and lots of other conscious choices come in. So what I am describing here is really just the entrance ramp for a long, long highway.

what love of god is not

In order for God's love to reach us, we much first love God. In other words, we can't acquire a virtue that we don't want. Bahá'u'lláh says this beautifully when He writes:

In order for God's love to reach us, we much first love God.

> O SON OF BEING! Love Me, that I may love thee. If thou lovest Me not, My love can in no wise reach thee. Know this, O servant. — *Bahá'u'lláh:*

God loves everyone. However, God's love cannot *reach* us unless we love God first. In other words, He cannot force us to accept a virtue as a sign of His love unless we are willing to live that virtue as a sign of our love for Him. Loving God and living virtue are identical activities.

Perhaps I shouldn't say it, but it seems pretty clear to me that there are millions of people in the world who think that they love God when they don't. Oh, they certainly love the *name* of God, and they love the *idea* of loving God, but the qualities that they have dedicated their lives to are *not* the qualities of God. They don't love peace. They don't love tolerance. They don't love anyone who doesn't agree that they are right. These are the people who hate in the name of God, who kill in the name of God, and who sow distrust and division in the name of righteousness. These are also the people who would joyfully consign the majority of the people in the world to a fiery hell in the name of God.

It is because of these people that 'Abdu'l-Bahá wrote:

Divine religion is not a cause for discord and disagreement. If religion becomes the source of antagonism and strife, the absence of religion is to be preferred. Religion is meant to be the quickening life of the body politic; if it be the cause of death to humanity, its nonexistence would be a blessing and benefit to man. — *'Abdu'l-Bahá*

These people, oddly enough, have a much clearer picture of God in their minds than I do. They worship a god that they know very well. Unfortunately, God—the *real* one—is unknowable in that way.

lovinG the unknowable

Perhaps now would be a good time to explain one of the great paradoxes of religion. You see, most religions tell us that we should love God and yet none of them has offered a very clear picture of what God is really like. Is He a "burning bush?" A "small still voice?" A "strong wind?" A giant man with a long beard? A powerful mind? There is a reason why none of these descriptions seem adequate, and that is that God is beyond our ability to comprehend. As 'Abdu'l-Bahá says:

We are no more able to understand the reality of God than a painting can understand the mind of its artist.

"That which we imagine, is not the Reality of God; He, the Unknowable, the Unthinkable, is far beyond the highest conception of man." — *'Abdu'l-Bahá*

We are no more able to understand the reality of God than a painting can understand the mind and creativity of its artist. Yet, having admitted that, there is a great deal that one can learn about an artist by looking at his creation. Likewise, we can learn a great deal about God by studying His greatest creation, the human soul. The important thing to keep in mind is that the *most perfect thing* that a human mind can imagine...is a perfect human mind. And God is very different from that. As a recent Christian song explained, trying to understand God is like trying to smell the color nine. We just don't have the tools needed.

Immeasurably exalted is His Essence above the descriptions of His creatures. He, alone, occupieth the Seat of transcendent majesty, of supreme and inaccessible glory. The birds of men's hearts, however high they soar, can never hope to attain the heights of His unknow-able Essence. — *Bahá'u'lláh*

Instead of spending our lives trying to turn mental somersaults, we have two perfectly good ways to learn more about God. One comes from studying the very best parts of ourselves—and that is our

We have two perfectly good ways to learn more about God.

virtues. As I just explained, when we explore our own soul, we are gazing into a mirror that is reflecting the human equivalent of the qualities of God. The other comes from observing the example and teachings of God's Prophets, who are as perfect mirrors. Between looking within and studying the lives and teaching of the Messengers of God, we have access to everything we will ever need to know on our path towards God.

UNDERSTANDING WHO WE ARE

So God is beyond our ability to comprehend, but one way we can learn about God is by studying the qualities of the human soul. This, then, would be a good time to tell you a little bit about this most wonderful of creations.

When I first explored the Bahá'í Faith, these were the teachings that interested me the most. It seems to me that if God went to all the trouble of creating me,

God placed something special within me, and it is my duty and blessing to discover what it is.

the least I could do is find out who I am, what my capacities are, and how to strive to achieve my highest potential. No matter how poorly people think of me, or how worthless I feel about myself, Bahá'u'lláh reminds me that He placed something special within me, and it is my duty and blessing to discover what it is. It may sound egocentric, but it really is the most important thing I am put here on earth to do. I certainly can't fulfill someone else's potential, and I can't develop a quality or virtue that I don't know I have.

Bahá'u'lláh's writings in this area are, in my opinion, some of the most beautiful, profound and inspiring ever revealed. Somehow they manage to evoke the loftiness of God while at the same time hinting at an intimate connection between man and God that sets my heart on fire.

O SON OF BEING! Thou art My lamp and My light is in thee. Get thou from it thy radiance and seek none other than Me. For I have created thee rich and have bountifully shed My favor upon thee.
— Bahá'u'lláh

Having created the world and all that liveth and moveth therein, He, through the direct operation of His unconstrained and sovereign Will, chose to confer upon man the unique distinction and capacity to know Him and to love Him—a capacity that must needs be regarded as the generating impulse and the primary purpose underlying the whole of creation.... Upon the inmost reality of each and every created thing He hath shed the light of one of His names, and made it a recipient of the glory of one of His attributes. Upon the reality of man, however, He hath focused the radiance of all of His names and attributes, and made it a mirror of His own Self. Alone of all created things man hath been singled out for so great a favor, so enduring a bounty.

These energies with which the Day Star of Divine bounty and Source of heavenly guidance hath endowed the reality of man lie, however, latent within him, even as the flame is hidden within the candle and the rays of light are potentially present in the lamp. The radiance of these energies may be obscured by worldly desires even as the light of the sun can be concealed beneath the dust and dross which cover the mirror. Neither the candle nor the lamp can be lighted through their own unaided efforts, nor can it ever be possible for the mirror to free itself from its dross. It is clear and evident that until a fire is kindled the lamp will never be ignited, and unless the dross is blotted out from the face of the mirror it can never represent the image of the sun nor reflect its light and glory. — *Bahá'u'lláh*

In case I didn't make it clear before, all of the things that I have been saying about discovering who I am and developing my true potential referred to my *spiritual* identity, not my body. In the Bahá'í Writings, the terms Mind, Soul and Spirit are often used interchangeably. They all refer to human qualities that are non-physical and eternal. If we were to make a distinction between them, we might say that the

The soul does not reside in the body, but is, rather, connected to it in the way that a beam of light is connected to the mirror that reflects it.

mind and rational soul are subsets of the spirit, which includes qualities and capacities that we are not necessarily conscious of. The soul does not reside *in* the body, but is, rather, connected to it in the way that a beam of light is connected to the mirror that reflects it. Through this connection, the soul is able to control the human body and experience the material world through physical senses. It would be a mistake, however, if we limited our-selves to our physical senses alone. We also have spiritual senses, imagination, creativity, memory and other capacities that allow us to discover truths beyond the physical realm. Here are some more "nuts & bolts" descriptions of the human soul. There are some more in the section on the afterlife.

In man five outer powers exist, which are the agents of percep-tion—that is to say, through these five powers man perceives material beings. These are sight, which perceives visible forms; hearing, which perceives audible sounds; smell, which perceives odors; taste, which perceives foods; and feeling, which is in all parts of the body and perceives tangible things. These five powers perceive outward exist-ences.

Man has also spiritual powers: imagination, which conceives things; thought, which reflects upon realities; comprehension, which comprehends realities; memory, which retains whatever man imag-ines, thinks and comprehends. The intermediary between the five outward powers and the inward powers is the sense which they possess in common—that is to say, the sense which acts between the outer and inner powers, conveys to the inward powers whatever the outer pow-ers discern. It is termed the common faculty, because it communi-cates between the outward and inward powers and thus is common to the outward and inward powers.

For instance, sight is one of the outer powers; it sees and perceives this flower, and conveys this perception to the inner power—the com-mon faculty—which transmits this perception to the power of imagi-nation, which in its turn conceives and forms this image and trans-mits it to the power of thought; the power of thought reflects and, having grasped the reality, conveys it to the power of comprehension; the comprehension, when it has comprehended it, delivers the image of the object perceived to the memory, and the memory keeps it in its repository.

The outward powers are five: the power of sight, of hearing, of taste, of smell and of feeling.

The inner powers are also five: the common faculty, and the powers of imagination, thought, comprehension and memory.

— 'Abdu'l-Bahá

OUR Relationship to the Material World

In addition to explaining the human soul's relationship with God, the Bahá'í Writings also tell us something about our place in the world of creation. We can learn about God's qualities and virtues by looking at ourselves, but we can also learn about ourselves *and* God by observing the rest of creation. We can use our God-given intelligence and perception to explore the material world because the material world *also* reflects God's qualities, but to a lesser degree and in a different way.

> *We can learn about ourselves and God by observing the rest of creation.*

> *Whatever is in the heavens and whatever is on the earth is a direct evidence of the revelation within it of the attributes and names of God, inasmuch as within every atom are enshrined the signs that bear eloquent testimony to the revelation of that Most Great Light.*

> *...From that which hath been said it becometh evident that all things, in their inmost reality, testify to the revelation of the names and attributes of God within them. Each according to its capacity, indicateth, and is expressive of, the knowledge of God.... Likewise hath the eternal King spoken: "No thing have I perceived, except that I perceived God within it, God before it, or God after it."*
> — Bahá'u'lláh

From this perspective, the world becomes a schoolhouse. It is not the realm of the "devil." It is not evil, but neither is it the final example of what we are striving for. We have to look beyond our animal qualities to discover our more subtle and spiritual capacities.

the question of good and evil

While I am touching on the subject of the relationship between the soul and the material world, let me explain a little bit
about the Bahá'í perspective on good and evil. For many people,
this could be the most important chapter in this book. I know it
would have been for me.

I started this book talking about the concept of salvation,
and how I couldn't believe that a loving God would damn people
to hell just for being sinful. I didn't question the fact that we
were all sinful, I just didn't think we deserved such severe punishment for being the people God created us to be.

God created me noble,
perfect, good and
complete from the
beginning.

It came as quite a shock, then, to
read that God had created me noble,
perfect, good and complete from the beginning. How could I end up so rotten
if I had been created good?

All beings, whether large or small, were created perfect and com-
plete from the first, but their perfections appear in them by degrees.
— 'Abdu'l-Bahá

The answer, quite simply, is that what appears to us to be evil
is simply the absence of good. Darkness has no independent
existence. It is only the absence of light. In more practical terms,
one dollar, compared to a million, is not a debt, but it certainly
is not as useful. We begin our lives as babies with the potential
capacity to express a million different virtues. If we only practice
one, we will appear pretty bad to our neighbors.

All of this may sound like a game of semantics, but it actually
makes a huge difference in the way people think about themselves. Consider the difference between stupidity and ignorance.
If you see yourself as stupid, then you don't believe that you are
capable of learning and therefore give up easily or don't try at all.

If you see yourself as ignorant but smart, then every experience is a learning opportunity. Life is exciting, and nothing can stop you from exploring new fields of knowledge.

When we believe that we are "born in iniquity and raised in sin," controlled by the devil, or cursed with original sin, evil tendencies and an aggressive nature, then acquiring virtues is no longer an opportunity, it is a doomed struggle from the beginning. Why should I try to behave in a way that I have been taught is contrary to my very nature? Why should I do battle with a devil whose will is stronger than my own?

The sad thing is that you don't even have to have been raised religious to carry these beliefs subconsciously. They are part of our culture, infused into our entertainment, and reinforced by our educational system. It does no good to either ignore or deny their influence on our behavior. What we need is a new, positive, rational and spiritually-coherent view of the human soul. This is what I found in the Bahá'í teachings.

Belief in original sin is part of our culture, infused into our entertainment, and reinforced by our educational system.

O SON OF BEING! With the hands of power I made thee and with the fingers of strength I created thee; and within thee have I placed the essence of My light. Be thou content with it and seek naught else, for My work is perfect and My command is binding. Question it not, nor have a doubt thereof. — Bahá'u'lláh

In creation there is no evil; all is good. Certain qualities and natures innate in some men and apparently blameworthy are not so in reality. For example, from the beginning of his life you can see in a nursing child the signs of greed, of anger and of temper. Then, it may be said, good and evil are innate in the reality of man, and this is contrary to the pure goodness of nature and creation. The answer to this is that greed, which is to ask for something more, is a praiseworthy quality provided that it is used suitably. So if a man is

35

*greedy to acquire science and knowledge, or to become compassion-
ate, generous and just, it is most praiseworthy. If he exercises his
anger and wrath against the bloodthirsty tyrants who are like fero-
cious beasts, it is very praiseworthy; but if he does not use these qualities in a right way, they are blameworthy.*

*Then it is evident that in creation and nature evil does not
exist at all; but when the natural qualities of man are used in an
unlawful way, they are blameworthy. So if a rich and generous
person gives a sum of money to a poor man for his own necessities,
and if the poor man spends that sum of money on unlawful things,
that will be blameworthy. It is the same with all the natural qualities of man, which constitute the capital of life; if they be used and
displayed in an unlawful way, they become
blameworthy. Therefore, it is clear that creation is purely good.* — *'Abdu'l-Bahá*

**The Bahá'í writings
offer a very positive
and inspiring vision
of our spiritual
station as humans.**

The above quotations, along with the
earlier ones about God's love and our
special capacities, combine to create a very
positive and inspiring vision of our spiritual station as humans. They were al-
most enough to make me feel serene, blessed, thankful, and (dare
I say it?) *saved*. But not right away. While I intellectually accepted all of these teachings the moment I heard them, it took
many years of prayer and meditation for the beliefs to sink into
my heart and change the way I *felt* about myself and my relationship with God. If you find yourself dealing with issues of shame,
depression, worthlessness, anger or even hopelessness, it is important to realize that these feelings are rooted in both your
belief system and your emotional environment. I believe you will
find that the Bahá'í Writings do a good job of speaking to both
your mind and your heart. This theme is explored further in the
book ***Why Me? A Spiritual Guide to Growing Through Tests***.
(See bibliography)

the afterlife

What happens after we die? Bahá'ís believe that the soul has a beginning, but no end, which means that our mortal lives are just a blink of an eye when compared to the eternity we will spend without a physical body. If you thought that trying to understand God was difficult, well, understanding what it will be like to exist without a body is not a whole lot easier. For the most part, Bahá'u'lláh tells us that it is impossible to imagine. On the other hand, there are some things that we *do* know simply because we will be taking our souls with us, and we *do* know a little bit about our souls.

To start, our spirits are not physical, so they are not bound by time or space. That fact *alone* should give you an idea of why it is impossible to imagine. We take our virtues and our capacities with us. We keep our personalities and our memories, and we will be able to recognize and communicate with other people. Soon after we die, we will experience a life-review. If we have developed our spiritual capacities then we will be allowed to use them in service to one another and God. Note that when I talk about spiritual capacities, I'm talking about the things Christians would call "fruits of the spirit" like love and faith, not sci-fi mind-over-matter powers.

Here are just a few of the Bahá'í Writings on this subject.

Some think that the body is the substance and exists by itself, and that the spirit is accidental and depends upon the substance of the body, although, on the contrary, the rational soul is the substance, and the body depends upon it. If the accident—that is to say, the body—be destroyed, the substance, the spirit, remains.

Second, the rational soul, meaning the human spirit, does not descend into the body—that is to say, it does not enter it, for descent and entrance are characteristics of bodies, and the rational soul is exempt from this. The spirit never entered this body, so in quitting it, it will not be in need of an abiding-place: no, the spirit is connected with the body, as this light is with this mirror. When the mirror is

clear and perfect, the light of the lamp will be apparent in it, and when the mirror becomes covered with dust or breaks, the light will disappear.

The rational soul—that is to say, the human spirit—has neither entered this body nor existed through it; so after the disintegration of the composition of the body, how should it be in need of a substance through which it may exist? On the contrary, the rational soul is the substance through which the body exists. The personality of the rational soul is from its beginning; it is not due to the instrumentality of the body, but the state and the personality of the rational soul may be strengthened in this world; it will make progress and will attain to the degrees of perfection, or it will remain in the lowest abyss of ignorance, veiled and deprived from beholding the signs of God.

— 'Abdu'l-Bahá

> **The purpose of this life is to prepare us for the afterlife in the same way as the nine months in the womb were designed to prepare us for our physical lives.**

A favorite Bahá'í analogy is to say that the purpose of this life is to prepare us for the afterlife in the same way as the nine months in the womb were designed to prepare us for our physical lives. Death is just as natural, and just as beautiful as birth. But if we do not prepare ourselves, we will be "spiritually handicapped" when we enter the next stage of our development.

The nature of the soul after death can never be described, nor is it meet and permissible to reveal its whole character to the eyes of men.... The world beyond is as different from this world as this world is different from that of the child while still in the womb of its mother. When the soul attaineth the Presence of God, it will assume the form that best befitteth its immortality and is worthy of its celestial habitation.   *— Bahá'u'lláh*

Thou hast asked Me whether man, as apart from the Prophets of God and His chosen ones, will retain, after his physical death, the self-same individuality, personality, consciousness, and understanding that characterize his life in this world....

Know thou that the soul of man is exalted above, and is independent of all infirmities of body or mind. That a sick person showeth signs of weakness is due to the hindrances that interpose themselves between his soul and his body, for the soul itself remaineth unaffected by any bodily ailments. Consider the light of the lamp. Though an external object may interfere with its radiance, the light itself continueth to shine with undiminished power. In like manner, every malady afflicting the body of man is an impediment that preventeth the soul from manifesting its inherent might and power. When it leaveth the body, however, it will evince such ascendancy, and reveal such influence as no force on earth can equal. Every pure, every refined and sanctified soul will be endowed with tremendous power, and shall rejoice with exceeding gladness. — Baha'u'llah

It is clear and evident that all men shall, after their physical death, estimate the worth of their deeds, and realize all that their hands have wrought. — Bahá'u'lláh

In all of these quotations about the afterlife, you may have noticed a subtle difference between them and the traditional view of heaven. Not only are the traditional harps, wings and clouds missing, but the static view of perfection has given way to a view of perfection in motion. Perfection is not seen as an end-point, it is a state of being in which we continue to move smoothly towards God.

In other words, the Bahá'í theme of *progress* appears in heaven just as it did in explaining the progressive nature of God's single, unfolding religion, and as it will again when we talk about the advancement of civilization.

The Bahá'í theme of progress *appears in heaven just as it did in explaining the progressive nature of religion.*

Thus it is established that this movement is necessary to existence, which is either growing or declining. Now, as the spirit continues to exist after death, it necessarily progresses or declines; and in the other world to cease to progress is the same as to decline; but it never leaves its own condition, in which it continues to develop. — 'Abdu'l-Bahá

✳ MY BAHÁ'Í FAITH

DEVELOPING OUR VIRTUES

There is a reason why I keep coming back to the subject of virtues. Virtues are the most down-to-earth way of talking about the goal of religion and spirituality. As I've already explained, the purpose of life is to acquire virtues. Virtues are how we express God's love and reflect God's love. Virtues are also the things that the Prophets of God teach us about and exemplify.

What are some of the virtues that Bahá'u'lláh and the Bahá'í Writings mention in specific? So, having said all of that, what are some of the virtues that Bahá'u'lláh and the Bahá'í Writings mention in specific? Well, as I said, all of God's Messengers have brought the same basic spiritual teachings, and yet it is also true that each religion offers a slightly different emphasis. Moses focused on obedience to laws. Jesus' primary message was about love. Mohammed taught submission to the Will of God. Buddha taught compassion, humility and detachment. Bahá'u'lláh exalted unity, purity, kindness, radiance and justice. Here are some Bahá'í Writings about virtues:

> *The Purpose of the one true God, exalted be His glory, in revealing Himself unto men is to lay bare those gems that lie hidden within the mine of their true and inmost selves.* — Bahá'u'lláh

> *All men have been created to carry forward an ever-advancing civilization. The Almighty beareth Me witness: To act like the beasts of the field is unworthy of man. Those virtues that befit his dignity are forbearance, mercy, compassion and loving-kindness towards all the peoples and kindreds of the earth. Say: O friends! Drink your fill from this crystal stream that floweth through the heavenly grace of Him Who is the Lord of Names. Let others partake of its waters in My name, that the leaders of men in every land may fully recognize the purpose for which the Eternal Truth hath been revealed, and the reason for which they themselves have been created.*
> — Bahá'u'lláh

Be generous in prosperity, and thankful in adversity. Be worthy of the trust of thy neighbor, and look upon him with a bright and friendly face. Be a treasure to the poor, an admonisher to the rich, an answerer of the cry of the needy, a preserver of the sanctity of thy pledge. Be fair in thy judgment, and guarded in thy speech. Be unjust to no man, and show all meekness to all men. Be as a lamp unto them that walk in darkness, a joy to the sorrowful, a sea for the thirsty, a haven for the distressed, an upholder and defender of the victim of oppression. Let integrity and uprightness distinguish all thine acts. Be a home for the stranger, a balm to the suffering, a tower of strength for the fugitive. Be eyes to the blind, and a guiding light unto the feet of the erring. Be an ornament to the countenance of truth, a crown to the brow of fidelity, a pillar of the temple of righteousness, a breath of life to the body of mankind, an ensign of the hosts of justice, a luminary above the horizon of virtue, a dew to the soil of the human heart, an ark on the ocean of knowledge, a sun in the heaven of bounty, a gem on the diadem of wisdom, a shining light in the firmament of thy generation, a fruit upon the tree of humility. — Bahá'u'lláh

> **"Be generous in prosperity, and thankful in adversity."**

But the spirit of man has two aspects: one divine, one satanic - that is to say, it is capable of the utmost perfection, or it is capable of the utmost imperfection. If it acquires virtues, it is the most noble of the existing beings; and if it acquires vices, it becomes the most degraded existence. — 'Abdu'l-Bahá

A Prayer for Virtues

O my Lord! Make Thy beauty to be my food, and Thy presence my drink, and Thy pleasure my hope, and praise of Thee my action, and remembrance of Thee my companion, and the power of Thy sovereignty my succorer, and Thy habitation my home, and my dwelling-place the seat Thou hast sanctified from the limitations imposed upon them who are shut out as by a veil from Thee.

Thou art, verily, the Almighty, the All-Glorious, the Most Powerful. — Bahá'u'lláh

✳ MY BAHÁ'Í FAITH

GROWING through tests

It is all well and good to like virtues, identify virtues and observe examples of virtues, but at some point, we have to actually live our virtues. I wish I could tell you that if you prayed a certain prayer or observed a particular ritual you would magically acquire virtues, but life doesn't work that way. Virtues are skills, and like every other skill we acquire—from learning to walk to working a computer—they take practice.

Virtues are skills, and like every other skill we acquire, they take practice. Sometimes we are fairly good at them, and sometimes we are not. That's when virtues become tests. A test, problem or difficulty is simply a situation in which a virtue is required. If you have the virtue,

then it is a small test. If you don't, then it can quickly become a very large test. Overcoming the test will almost always strengthen your virtues for the next time you need them. That is why every major religion has challenged common wisdom and insisted that difficulties are good. Here is the Bahá'í perspective:

O SON OF MAN! My calamity is My providence, outwardly it is fire and vengeance, but inwardly it is light and mercy. Hasten thereunto that thou mayest become an eternal light and an immortal spirit. This is My command unto thee, do thou observe it.
— *Bahá'u'lláh*

Men who suffer not, attain no perfection. The plant most pruned by the gardeners is that one which, when the summer comes, will have the most beautiful blossoms and the most abundant fruit.
— *'Abdu'l-Bahá*

The more difficulties one sees in the world the more perfect one becomes. The more you plough and dig the ground the more fertile it becomes. The more you put the gold in the fire the purer it becomes. The more you sharpen the steel by grinding the better it cuts. Therefore, the more sorrows one sees the more perfect one becomes. That is

42

why, in all times, the Prophets of God have had tribulations and difficulties to withstand. The more often the captain of a ship is on the tempest and difficult sailing the greater his knowledge becomes. Therefore I am happy that you have had great tribulation and difficulties. For this I am very happy—that you have had many sorrows. Strange it is that I love you and still I am happy that you have sorrows. —'Abdu'l-Bahá

The good side of this approach to difficulties is that it helps relieve some of the feelings of shame, guilt, unworthiness, and punishment that often accompany personal tests. Without these negative associations, we are more likely to turn to God and to each other for help and support. Realizing that tests are gifts from God, we can rest assured that, when we are ready for them, the virtues, understanding and support we need to overcome the tests will come from the same Source.

Tests are gifts from God to help us acquire more virtues.

The bad side of this approach is that we never get to justify wallowing in self-pity or resentment. For some of us, that is a real test in and of itself!

A Prayer for Times of Tests:

O God! Refresh and gladden my spirit. Purify my heart. Illumine my powers. I lay all my affairs in Thy hand. Thou art my Guide and my Refuge. I will no longer be sorrowful and grieved; I will be a happy and joyful being. O God! I will no longer be full of anxiety, nor will I let trouble harass me. I will not dwell on the unpleasant things of life.

O God! Thou art more friend to me than I am to myself. I dedicate myself to Thee, O Lord.

— 'Abdu'l-Bahá

PRAYER AND MEDITATION

Two of the greatest tools we have for overcoming tests and developing our virtues are prayer and meditation. To be honest, when I first became a Bahá'í, I didn't really understand the concept of prayer. I mean, how do you talk with an unknowable God? Are you really talking to God or are you talking to Him through one of the Prophets—or even an angel? Is anyone listening? Why would God care if we took time out of our day to say thank you and tell Him how great He is?

Thirty years later, I still am not sure about the grand metaphysical questions. I have some ideas, but ultimately I've decided that it doesn't really matter how far into "heaven" my prayers fly or where they land. What is important is the direction that I send them. You see, I have absolutely no control over what happens after my prayers leave my heart. I can only control my intention, my purity, and the degree to which I align my heart with the virtues of God. So prayer is mostly about mentally and spiritually aligning myself with God. It is about being receptive, and it causes good things to become attracted to us.

Prayer is mentally and spiritually aligning myself with God, and being receptive.

How does that work?

Think of God's love as an attractive force—a magnetic force, if you will. It lends power to those things that are aligned with it and draws them to it. Now imagine your own soul like a piece of steel. A piece of steel is made up of atoms—each of which is a tiny magnet with a positive and negative pole. Likewise, every part of you—your personality and character, your thoughts and feelings—are capable of turning towards virtues and being aligned with God. In practice, however, your different parts are pointed every which-way. Money, sex, success, pleasure, food and many other distractions pull your inner qualities away from alignment with God.

The word of God, whether it is in the form of a prayer or other sacred Scripture, acts as a magnet on the cold steel of your soul. Have you every touched a magnet to a nail and watched what happens? The entire nail becomes a magnet while they are in contact.

But here is the exciting part. Have you seen what the long-term effect of a powerful magnet can be on a lowly nail? Over time, the magnet permanently realigns some of the atoms of the nail so that eventually the nail it-self can become a powerful magnet.

The word of God acts as a magnet on the cold steel of your soul.

Every time we pray, we align ourselves with God. We touch the infinite and then let go... We touch the infinite and then let go. At first the effect is literally microscopic, but in time, all of those microscopic elements of our soul begin to align with the Will of God—and with each other! We become magnetic and spiritually attractive. Our virtues begin to have an influence on our surroundings by drawing out the virtues and positive emo-tions of the people around us.

Lets look at a typical Bahá'í prayer and see what I mean:

O God, my God! Aid Thou Thy trusted servants to have loving and tender hearts. Help them to spread, amongst all the nations of the earth, the light of guidance that cometh from the Company on high. Verily Thou art the Strong, the Powerful, the Mighty, the All-Subduing, the Ever-Giving. Verily Thou art the Generous, the Gentle, the Tender, the Most Bountiful. — 'Abdu'l-Bahá

What an incredible prayer. In sixty-two words, 'Abdu'l-Bahá sets a tone that makes every atom of my soul long to align itself with such universal virtues as tenderness, guidance, strength, gen-erosity, gentleness and bounty. Using his words, I call myself trusted and assure myself that even the angels in heaven (the Company on high) are aligned with my highest purpose, which is service to all the world.

45

Though Bahá'ís consider the prayers of Bahá'u'lláh and 'Abdu'l-Bahá especially "attractive," the act of saying *any* prayer—particularly one that comes from the depths of your own heart—will cause your soul to align itself with the virtues for which you express a longing. If you pray for wisdom and serenity, then your soul will be aligned with them. If, however, you pray for a million dollars, a parking space or vengeance against your enemy, then that is what you are aligning yourself with. Who knows, you might get them. But they are not what God wants you to want. That is why it is useful to at least familiarize ourselves with the prayers contained in the Sacred Writings. Prayers like the Lord's Prayer and the Bahá'í prayers help train us to know what to ask for so that when we *do* pray from the heart, our hearts are already aligned with God's Will for us.

Saying Bahá'í prayers makes me *want* to develop virtues, and my desire for virtue is what keeps me aligned with God even after the prayer is over—which brings me to the next step.

Saying a prayer and not meditating is like asking God a question and not listening for an answer.

meditation

Saying a prayer and not meditating afterwards is like asking God a question and then not listening for an answer. But where do the answers come from? Well, if someone tells me that God whispers in his or her ears, I would not want to argue with them. I've seen God work in mysterious ways. But for those of us whose cell phone connection is not quite so clear, I would like to offer some alternative understandings of the value of meditation.

First, meditation that follows prayer allows the soul to linger in a state of attraction and alignment. If you've ever taken the time to magnetize a piece of steel and then accidentally dropped it on the floor, you know the disappointment of losing the power of attraction because of the jarring effect of contact with cold hard reality.

Second, many people pray in search of guidance during times of trouble. As I explained in the section on tests, difficulties help us to grow by developing our virtues. I can pretty much guarantee that the answer to your prayers will involve the application of one or more virtues. Virtue attracts virtue. When we pray and align ourselves with the virtues of God that are expressed in our prayers, we become more attracted to and aware of all of the other virtues of God. Meditation after prayer allows our souls to identify and become attracted to the virtues we need to solve our problems. We are also taking the time to imagine ways to put abstract virtues into concrete action.

Finally, being aligned with the virtues of God feels good. If we rush straight from prayer to action, we don't take the time to enjoy the spiritual sensations associated with feeling the attractive power of the good. In other words, we deprive ourselves of feeling the love of God.

Please understand that all of this is just my personal take on prayer and meditation. The Bahá'í Writings allow for a wide range of understandings. You are welcome to read one of the many Bahá'í books on the subject, or, better yet, discover your own insights. Here are some quotations to get you started.

Intone, O My servants, the verses of God that have been received by thee, as intoned by them who have drawn nigh unto Him, that the sweetness of thy melody may kindle thine own soul, and attract the hearts of all men. Whoso reciteth, in the privacy of his chamber, the verses revealed by God, the scattering angels of the Almighty shall scatter abroad the fragrance of the words uttered by his mouth, and shall cause the heart of every righteous man to throb. Though he may, at first, remain unaware of its effect, yet the virtue of the grace vouchsafed unto him must needs sooner or later exercise its influence upon his soul. Thus have the mysteries of the Revelation of God been decreed by virtue of the Will of Him Who is the Source of power and wisdom. — *Bahá'u'lláh*

Know thou, verily, it is becoming in a weak one to supplicate to the Strong One, and it behooveth a seeker of bounty to beseech the Glorious Bountiful One. When one supplicates to his Lord, turns to Him and seeks bounty from His Ocean, this supplication brings light to his heart, illumination to his sight, life to his soul and exaltation to his being.

During thy supplications to God and thy reciting, "Thy Name is my healing," consider how thine heart is cheered, thy soul delighted by the spirit of the love of God, and thy mind attracted to the Kingdom of God! By these attractions one's ability and capacity increase. When the vessel is enlarged the water increases, and when the thirst grows the bounty of the cloud becomes agreeable to the taste of man. This is the mystery of supplication and the wisdom of stating one's wants.

— 'Abdu'l-Bahá:

It is an axiomatic fact that while you meditate you are speaking with your own spirit. In that state of mind you put certain questions to your spirit and the spirit answers: the light breaks forth and the reality is revealed....

The meditative faculty is akin to the mirror; if you put it before earthly objects it will reflect them. Therefore if the spirit of man is contemplating earthly subjects he will be informed of these.

But if you turn the mirror of your spirits heavenwards, the heavenly constellations and the rays of the Sun of Reality will be reflected in your hearts, and the virtues of the Kingdom will be obtained.

— 'Abdu'l-Bahá

TOOLS FOR SOCIAL PROGRESS

Up until now, I have focused on the more personal aspects of the Bahá'í teachings. This is the aspect of religion that most people are familiar with *and* most comfortable with. But Bahá'u'lláh explains that our purpose in life is three-fold. We are to love God, acquire virtues, and *carry forward an ever-advancing civilization.*

To many people, advancing civilization is the job of science and politics, not religion. But for Bahá'ís, progress and growth are central to God's great plan for humanity. While each Prophet taught

Progress and growth are central to God's great plan for humanity.

the same essential virtues, they also taught us how to apply those virtues in progressively broader and more complex areas of life. Bahá'ís talk about these two aspects of religion as the spiritual and the social teachings.

Each of the divine religions embodies two kinds of ordinances. The first is those which concern spiritual susceptibilities, the development of moral principles and the quickening of the conscience of man. These are essential or fundamental, one and the same in all religions, changeless and eternal - reality not subject to transformation. Abraham heralded this reality, Moses promulgated it, and Jesus Christ established it in the world of mankind. All the divine Prophets and Messengers were the instruments and channels of this same eternal, essential truth.

The second kind of ordinances in the divine religions is those which relate to the material affairs of humankind. These are the material or accidental laws which are subject to change in each day of manifestation, according to exigencies of the time, conditions and differing capacities of humanity. — 'Abdu'l-Bahá

49

THE NEED FOR NEW SOCIAL TEACHINGS

I already explained the idea that the human race was entering a new stage of maturity, and discussed some of the implications for our personal relationship with God. Individual maturity allows a new relationship with God, while collective maturity allows a new relationship between peoples and nations. Yes, we continue to make mistakes and behave like spoiled children much of the time. But we also have flashes of brilliance, moments of maturity, and great prospects for peace.

The Bahá'í era began, coincidentally, on the same day that the first telegraph message was sent. On that day, the world shrank. We acquired the technological tools we need to create an interconnected and interdependent global community. We can see that science, travel and communication have caused diverse races, religions, nations and cultures to overlap and interact as never before. Because of this, we also need guidance as to how to make this interconnected community a unified, cooperative and loving community. We must learn how to demonstrate personal virtues on a social scale. We need tools for resolving differences and principles that bridge cultural divides. This is why God chose *this* time to send a new teacher.

We must learn how to demonstrate personal virtues on a social scale.

The social teachings that Bahá'u'lláh offered the world provide a moral framework on which a diverse yet cohesive global community can be built. It outlines basic human rights, explains universal spiritual principles and provides specific tools for moving the world forward. Even more important, these teachings create a spiritual environment that helps release human potential and inspire visionary action.

Here, in their short form, are some of the basic principles:

One God
One Religion
One Human Race
Elimination of Prejudice
Equality of Women and Men
Harmony of Science & Religion
World Peace
World Government
World Language
Economic Justice
Consultation

At first glance, this list of Bahá'í social teachings may not seem all that evolutionary. You have probably heard most of them before. They were radical back in the 1800's but they are considered fairly obvious now.

What this list misses; what it fails to capture, is the great, cosmic, world-embracing vision that makes you want to stand up and cheer with joy and gratitude once you finally "get it."

Bahá'u'lláh invites us to look at the world through God's eyes and see our glorious destiny. God created us as one planet and one human race. God has been patiently educating us, millennium after millennium, until we are finally ready to come together as brothers and sisters. There is no need to fight. There is no need to compete. We are not innately evil, aggressive, violent or selfish. We were created *by* Love in order to *express* love. We are invited to discover our infinite, untapped potential to love each other, take care of each other, and create a beautiful world together. This is not pie-in-the-sky wishful thinking. This is a logical, coherent perspective that flows directly from the realization that God loves all of us equally. If there is a God, then this *has to be* where the world is headed.

Once you adopt this vision, then the basic principles are no longer abstract political positions, they are obvious extensions of the path towards the end goal. We don't just believe in the elimination of prejudice; we believe in the God-given value of every human, and love them as equal participants in this exciting process of growth. World peace is not just an end to war, it is the first logical step in the progress towards universal brotherhood (and sisterhood). Auxiliary language? It is simply a tool to make it easier to communicate with all of the wonderful and diverse people in the world.

There is a difference between promoting social principles as a political agenda, and living them as a spiritual truth.

What the last thirty years have demonstrated to me is that there is a difference between promoting social principles as a political agenda, and living them as a spiritual truth. For example, I used to think that when everyone came to believe in peace, we would have peace. Well, politicians have *said* that they believed in peace for over half a century, yet we have not achieved it. This is because we have not nurtured the love of peace *in our hearts* where it would actually make a difference. It is in our hearts that social principles become spiritual reality.

As you read the quotations in the following sections, think about how these ideas might be presented if they were being discussed in a political setting, then compare that to the way in which Bahá'u'lláh and 'Abdu'l-Bahá present them as an expression of the Will of God. Pay attention to how each principle is explained in relation to the greater vision. When the heart is inspired by the vision of what is possible, then the mind is better able to understand and apply the principle.

LOVING EACH OTHER

There is probably no social/spiritual principle that is more widely accepted and yet universally ignored than the call to love one another. Bahá'u'lláh offers more than just a few more well-phrased platitudes on the subject. Love is a conscious choice, an active force, a logical extension of our inner reality, and an attractive alternative to division and hatred. It is the foundation of our vision of a united world. The Bahá'í Writings address the "who, how, when where and why" of the social application of the spiritual principle of love. Here is a sampling of what they have to say:

Ye are the fruits of one tree, and the leaves of one branch. Deal ye one with another with the utmost love and harmony, with friendliness and fellowship. He Who is the Day-Star of Truth beareth Me witness! So powerful is the light of unity that it can illuminate the whole earth. — *Bahá'u'lláh*

Wish not for others what ye wish not for yourselves; fear God, and be not of the prideful. Ye are all created out of water, and unto dust shall ye return. Reflect upon the end that awaiteth you, and walk not in the ways of the oppressor. — *Bahá'u'lláh*

The earth is but one country, and mankind its citizens. — *Bahá'u'lláh*

God has created His servants in order that they may love and associate with each other. He has revealed the glorious splendor of His sun of love in the world of humanity. The cause of the creation of the phenomenal world is love. — *'Abdu'l-Bahá*

God desires unity and love; He commands harmony and fellowship. Enmity is human disobedience; God Himself is love. — *'Abdu'l-Bahá*

Consider how kind Jesus Christ was, that even upon the cross He prayed for His oppressors. We must follow His example. We must emulate the Prophets of God. We must follow Jesus Christ. We must free ourselves from all these imitations which are the source of darkness in the world. — *'Abdu'l-Baha*

✳ MY BAHÁ'Í FAITH

ELIMINATING PREJUDICE

One of the first tests of our ability to apply the principle of love comes when we encounter people who are observably different from ourselves. While it has become politically correct to support interracial understanding, tolerance and diversity in the last forty years or so, the Bahá'í Community has set its sights on a higher goal for over a hundred years. We are encouraged to love, become best friends with, and even intermarry with people of every racial, cultural, religious and ethnic background. And we do. We keep our "eye on the prize" because we have a vision of what America and the world would look like without the shackles of prejudice holding us back.

Racial prejudice, in particular, is considered America's "most challenging issue."

Racial prejudice, in particular, is considered America's "most challenging issue," and the American Bahá'í Community has taken a proactive approach to addressing it. I won't pretend that we have done a perfect job of it, but through literature, workshops, conferences, celebrations and institutes thousands of Bahá'ís of many races have made conscious efforts to bring about understanding and true friendships among each other.

O CHILDREN OF MEN! Know ye not why We created you all from the same dust? That no one should exalt himself over the other. Ponder at all times in your hearts how ye were created. Since We have created you all from one same substance it is incumbent on you to be even as one soul, to walk with the same feet, eat with the same mouth and dwell in the same land, that from your inmost being, by your deeds and actions, the signs of oneness and the essence of detachment may be made manifest. Such is My counsel to you, O concourse of light! Heed ye this counsel that ye may obtain the fruit of holiness from the tree of wondrous glory. — *Bahá'u'lláh*

. . . prejudice - whether it be religious, racial, patriotic or political in its origin and aspect - is the destroyer of human foundations and opposed to the commands of God. ('Abdu'l-Bahá:

And the breeding-ground of all these tragedies is prejudice: prejudice of race and nation, of religion, of political opinion; and the root cause of prejudice is blind imitation of the past - imitation in religion, in racial attitudes, in national bias, in politics. So long as this aping of the past persisteth, just so long will the foundations of the social order be blown to the four winds, just so long will humanity be continually exposed to direst peril. — 'Abdu'l-Bahá:

But there is need of a superior power to overcome human prejudices, a power which nothing in the world of mankind can withstand and which will overshadow the effect of all other forces at work in human conditions. That irresistible power is the love of God. It is my hope and prayer that it may destroy the prejudice of this one point of distinction between you and unite you all permanently under its hallowed protection. — 'Abdu'l-Bahá

Your eyes have been illumined, your ears are attentive, your hearts knowing. You must be free from prejudice and fanaticism, beholding no differences between the races and religions. You must look to God, for He is the real Shepherd, and all humanity are His sheep. He loves them and loves them equally. As this is true, should the sheep quarrel among themselves? They should manifest gratitude and thankfulness to God, and the best way to thank God is to love one another. — 'Abdu'l-Bahá

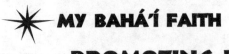

MY BAHÁ'Í FAITH

PROMOTING PEACE

Peace is a real hot-button issue these days, so it is helpful to remember that Bahá'ís have been promoting non-violent conflict resolution for over 160 years. We are not pacifists in the traditional sense of the word because we understand that defensive and protective actions are sometimes necessary as a last resort. On the other hand, Bahá'ís have been working to create a global environment that will heal the causes of war. We also support international institutions that will reduce its likelihood.

Bahá'ís have identified racial, ethnic, political and *religious* prejudices as the root causes of war and have dedicated themselves to helping the entire world see itself as one country and one human family. Only when this larger vision is accepted by the political and religious leaders of the world and incorporated into the school curricula of every country will we be able to make lasting progress towards the goal of peace.

Bahá'ís have dozens of specific ideas and proposals for how to promote peace on a local, national and international scale, but to me the most important gift the Bahá'í Writings have to offer is the assurance that peace is not only possible, but inevitable. God has been promising that humanity would eventually live in peace since before the time of Isaiah. God keeps His promises. We are not too evil and violent to live in peace, we are too immature. But immaturity does not have to be fatal, and it certainly doesn't have to be permanent. In fact, it usually isn't. When we believe that peace is possible, we behave differently. We work with more confidence and we live with less fear. These days, living with less fear would be a real blessing. Listen to the confidence expressed in the following quotations. They identify the problem, raise the discussion to a spiritual level, offer a vision of what is to come, and provide keys to the solution.

When love is realized and the ideal spiritual bonds unite the hearts of men, the whole human race will be uplifted, the world will continually grow more spiritual and radiant and the happiness and tranquillity of mankind be immeasurably increased. Warfare and strife will be uprooted, disagreement and dissension pass away and universal peace unite the nations and peoples of the world.

— 'Abdu'l-Bahá

All mankind are creatures and servants of the one God. The surface of the earth is one home; humanity is one family and household. Distinctions and boundaries are artificial, human. Why should there be discord and strife among men? All must become united and coordinated in service to the world of humanity.

— 'Abdu'l-Bahá

In the days of old an instinct for warfare was developed in the struggle with wild animals; this is no longer necessary; nay, rather, co-operation and mutual understanding are seen to produce the greatest welfare of mankind. Enmity is now the result of prejudice only.

— 'Abdu'l-Bahá

True civilization will unfurl its banner in the midmost heart of the world whenever a certain number of its distinguished and high-minded sovereigns—the shining exemplars of devotion and determination—shall, for the good and happiness of all mankind, arise, with firm resolve and clear vision, to establish the Cause of Universal Peace. They must make the Cause of Peace the object of general consultation, and seek by every means in their power to establish a Union of the nations of the world.

— 'Abdu'l-Bahá

The world is in greatest need of international peace. Until it is established, mankind will not attain composure and tranquillity. It is necessary that the nations and governments organize an international tribunal to which all their disputes and differences shall be referred. The decision of that tribunal shall be final. Individual controversy will be adjudged by a local tribunal. International questions will come before the universal tribunal, and so the cause of warfare will be taken away.

— 'Abdu'l-Bahá

The Great Peace towards which people of good will throughout the centuries have inclined their hearts, of which seers and poets for countless generations have expressed their vision, and for which from age to age the sacred scriptures of mankind have constantly held the promise, is now at long last within the reach of the nations. For the first time in history it is possible for everyone to view the entire planet, with all its myriad diversified peoples, in one perspective. World peace is not only possible but inevitable. It is the next stage in the evolution of this planet—in the words of one great thinker, "the planetization of mankind".   — The Universal House of Justice

This last quotation is the first paragraph from a document called *The Promise of World Peace*. If peace is a topic of special interest to you, then I encourage you to ask a Bahá'í for a copy of it. It presents the problem of where we've been, the vision of where we are going, and the path from one to the other with such clarity and insight that it will cheer your heart and give you hope just to read it.

SUPPORTING FAMILIES

It might seem strange to change topics from world peace to supporting families, but it is my way of reminding you (and me) that the same human virtues are needed at every level of interaction. Families are the foundation of civilization and of virtues.

Imagine a world in which every family was a safe and loving haven; in which children were seen as reflections of God, not sinful creatures; in which prejudice was never taught; in which people were considered more valuable than possessions; in which virtues were more important than looks or athletic ability; in which love of service was a greater motivator than fear of punishment. I won't pretend that Bahá'ís are living in that world yet, but I do believe that they are moving closer to it with every generation. The Bahá'í perspective encourages us to lean in that direction, and the Bahá'í teachings give us tools to help us achieve it. Prayers, guidance, insights, community support, and even a few rules here and there, help us become better parents and more united families.

My home is the home of peace. My home is the home of joy and delight. My home is the home of laughter and exultation. Whosoever enters through the portals of this home, must go out with gladsome heart. This is the home of light; whosoever enters here must become illumined.... — *'Abdu'l-Bahá*

The friends of God must so live and conduct themselves, and evince such excellence of character and conduct, as to make others astonished. The love between husband and wife must not be purely physical, nay, rather, it must be spiritual and heavenly. — *'Abdu'l-Bahá*

Note ye how easily, where unity existeth in a given family, the affairs of that family are conducted; what progress the members of that family make, how they prosper in the world. Their concerns are in order, they enjoy comfort and tranquillity, they are secure, their position is assured, they come to be envied by all. — *'Abdu'l-Bahá*

✳ MY BAHÁ'Í FAITH

According to the teachings of Bahá'u'lláh the family, being a human unit, must be educated according to the rules of sanctity. All the virtues must be taught the family. The integrity of the family bond must be constantly considered, and the rights of the individual members must not be transgressed. The rights of the son, the father, the mother - none of them must be transgressed, none of them must be arbitrary. Just as the son has certain obligations to his father, the father, likewise, has certain obligations to his son. The mother, the sister and other members of the household have their certain prerogatives. All these rights and prerogatives must be conserved, yet the unity of the family must be sustained. The injury of one shall be considered the injury of all; the comfort of each, the comfort of all; the honor of one, the honor of all. — 'Abdu'l-Bahá

SUPPORTING WOMEN

It is a logical observation that if children see one parent acting superior to or dominating another, they will naturally internalize the belief that some people are more important and more valuable than others. Therefore, equality of men and women in the family is the prerequisite foundation for a society in which equality is recognized for all people.

If children see one parent dominating another, they will naturally believe that some people are more important than others.

Another logical observation is that if we see ourselves as souls reflected in the material realm, rather than biological creatures trapped by our hormones and DNA, then it is clear that there is no *spiritual* difference between women and men. Equality is already a spiritual reality. It is only on the material level that inequalities still persist.

A final logical observation is that, since women have been denied equal education, opportunity and rights, for thousands of years, the world has been running on half its cylinders, so to speak. Or in more poetic terms, humanity has been like a bird with one bound wing. We will all progress much faster when both halves of humanity apply their full talents and potential to the problems we face.

What may be less obvious is how radical these observations seemed when they were first proclaimed in the mid 1800's. Women could not vote, nor could they own property separate from their husbands anywhere in the world. In the Middle East, where Bahá'u'lláh was writing, the situation was even worse than in the West. It is natural to assume that the progress made since then has been primarily due to political forces, but Bahá'ís believe that a larger plan of God has set these changes in motion.

Since women have been denied equal rights, for thousands of years, humanity has been like a bird with one bound wing.

Here is what God's latest chapter in the book of revelation has to say about the role and station of women in the world.

Women and men have been and will always be equal in the sight of God. The Dawning-Place of the Light of God sheddeth its radiance upon all with the same effulgence. Verily God created women for men, and men for women. — Bahá'u'lláh

And among the teachings of Baha'u'llah is the equality of women and men. The world of humanity has two wings - one is women and the other men. Not until both wings are equally developed can the bird fly. Should one wing remain weak, flight is impossible. Not until the world of women becomes equal to the world of men in the acquisition of virtues and perfections, can success and prosperity be attained as they ought to be. — 'Abdu'l-Bahá

Woman's lack of progress and proficiency has been due to her need of equal education and opportunity. Had she been allowed this equality, there is no doubt she would be the counterpart of man in ability and capacity. The happiness of mankind will be realized when women and men coordinate and advance equally, for each is the complement and helpmeet of the other. — 'Abdu'l-Bahá

✳ MY BAHÁ'Í FAITH
ENCOURAGING EDUCATION

I started this book talking about "salvation" as a result of spiritual education, so it should come as no surprise that education is a central principle of the Bahá'í Faith. It is such an important subject that I am going to break this section down into four parts: The importance of education in general; the need for each individual to seek out truth and understanding for themselves; the harmony of science and religion (i.e. material education and spiritual education); and the importance of applying that education to a field of service through work.

You will notice again that interwoven into the quotations about education are themes of God's love for us, the nobility of humanity, the joys of understanding and the eternal progress of the soul.

the importance of education

Man is the supreme Talisman. Lack of a proper education hath, however, deprived him of that which he doth inherently possess. Through a word proceeding out of the mouth of God he was called into being; by one word more he was guided to recognize the Source of his education; by yet another word his station and destiny were safeguarded. The Great Being saith: Regard man as a mine rich in gems of inestimable value. Education can, alone, cause it to reveal its treasures, and enable mankind to benefit therefrom.

— *Bahá'u'lláh*

Among other teachings and principles Bahá'u'lláh counsels the education of all members of society. No individual should be denied or deprived of intellectual training, although each should receive according to capacity. None must be left in the grades of ignorance, for ignorance is a defect in the human world. All mankind must be given a knowledge of science and philosophy - that is, as much as may be deemed necessary. All cannot be scientists and philosophers, but each should be educated according to his needs and deserts.

— *'Abdu'l-Bahá:*

Let the mothers consider that whatever concerneth the education of children is of the first importance. Let them put forth every effort in this regard, for when the bough is green and tender it will grow in whatever way ye train it. Therefore is it incumbent upon the mothers to rear their little ones even as a gardener tendeth his young plants. Let them strive by day and by night to establish within their children faith and certitude, the fear of God, the love of the Beloved of the worlds, and all good qualities and traits. Whensoever a mother seeth that her child hath done well, let her praise and applaud him and cheer his heart; and if the slightest undesirable trait should manifest itself, let her counsel the child and punish him, and use means based on reason, even a slight verbal chastisement should this be necessary. It is not, however, permissible to strike a child, or vilify him, for the child's character will be totally perverted if he be subjected to blows or verbal abuse. — 'Abdu'l-Bahá

seeking the truth

Blessed are the just souls who seek the truth. — 'Abdu'l-Bahá

Have you ever been in a religious setting in which you felt your questions were either discouraged or answered unsatisfactorily? If so, then you will appreciate the idea that not only should we seek the truth, but we should do so independently of other people's opinions and pressures. We are ultimately responsible for our own soul's progress.

We are ultimately responsible for our own soul's progress.

Happy is the man that pondereth in his heart that which hath been revealed in the Books of God, the Help in Peril, the Self-Subsisting. — Bahá'u'lláh

And now, concerning thy question regarding the creation of man. Know thou that all men have been created in the nature made by God, the Guardian, the Self-Subsisting. Unto each one hath been prescribed a pre-ordained measure, as decreed in God's mighty and guarded Tablets. All that which ye potentially possess can, however, be manifested only as a result of your own volition. Your own acts testify to this truth. — Bahá'u'lláh

63

God has given man the eye of investigation by which he may see and recognize truth. He has endowed man with ears that he may hear the message of reality and conferred upon him the gift of reason by which he may discover things for himself. This is his endowment and equipment for the investigation of reality. Man is not intended to see through the eyes of another, hear through another's ears nor comprehend with another's brain. Each human creature has individual endowment, power and responsibility in the creative plan of God. Therefore, depend upon your own reason and judgment and adhere to the outcome of your own investigation; otherwise, you will be utterly submerged in the sea of ignorance and deprived of all the bounties of God. — 'Abdu'l-Bahá

uniting science & religion

Interestingly, of all the basic Bahá'í principles, this is the one that surprises many people the most. Our culture is so used to separating our minds from our hearts, our reason from our faith, that it is exciting to find a religion that actually encourages the application of scientific principles to the study of spiritual truth.

I said earlier that, unaided by God's teachers, we could not discover spiritual truths simply by observing the world of nature and instinct. That might lead you to believe that we cannot study spiritual truths through scientific means. No. It only means that we can't study something without an example of it first. Once Moses or Jesus or Bahá'u'lláh lives a virtue that we can see, then we can study the results of that virtue in the human realm. We can study the effects of prayer, the influence of kindness or the effectiveness of generosity on the progress of the world. If we did that, then our faith would be based upon conscious knowledge.

The other side of this principle is the fact that minds which are unfettered by superstition, filled with joy, and appreciative of the perfection of God's creation are better equipped to discover new wonders in the material world. The harmony of science and religion will serve to deepen faith and energize science.

And among the teachings of Bahá'u'lláh is that religion must be in conformity with science and reason, so that it may influence the hearts of men. The foundation must be solid and must not consist of imitations. — *'Abdu'l-Bahá*

If religion is opposed to reason and science, faith is impossible; and when faith and confidence in the divine religion are not manifest in the heart, there can be no spiritual attainment.
— *'Abdu'l-Bahá*

Between scientists and the followers of religion there has always been controversy and strife for the reason that the latter have proclaimed religion superior in authority to science and considered scientific announcement opposed to the teachings of religion. Bahá'u'lláh declared that religion is in complete harmony with science and reason. If religious belief and doctrine is at variance with reason, it proceeds from the limited mind of man and not from God; therefore, it is unworthy of belief and not deserving of attention; the heart finds no rest in it, and real faith is impossible. How can man believe that which he knows to be opposed to reason? Is this possible? Can the heart accept that which reason denies? Reason is the first faculty of man, and the religion of God is in harmony with it. Bahá'u'lláh has removed this form of dissension and discord from among mankind and reconciled science with religion by revealing the pure teachings of the divine reality. This accomplishment is specialized to Him in this Day. — *'Abdu'l-Bahá*

Religion must conform to science and reason; otherwise, it is superstition. God has created man in order that he may perceive the verity of existence and endowed him with mind or reason to discover truth. Therefore, scientific knowledge and religious belief must be conformable to the analysis of this divine faculty in man.
— *'Abdu'l-Bahá*

WORK IS WORSHIP

So what is the point of all of this education, investigation and science? The point is that we develop our virtues—virtues that are practiced through service in the material world. In other words, Bahá'ís don't lock themselves away in monasteries, live in caves or separate themselves from the rest of civilization. We believe in applying our virtues through good old-fashioned work—whether that work takes place in the home or out. In doing so, we believe that we are both being of service *and* worshiping God at the same time. In other words, not only do we pray every day, but, for us, every day is a prayer.

In addition to this wide-spread education each child must be taught a profession, art, or trade, so that every member of the community will be enabled to earn his own livelihood. Work done in the spirit of service is the highest form of worship.... — *'Abdu'l-Bahá*

This is worship: to serve mankind and to minister to the needs of the people. Service is prayer. A physician ministering to the sick, gently, tenderly, free from prejudice and believing in the solidarity of the human race, he is giving praise'. — *'Abdu'l-Bahá*

It must not be implied that one should give up avocation and attainment to livelihood. On the contrary, in the Cause of Bahá'u'lláh monasticism and asceticism are not sanctioned. In this great Cause the light of guidance is shining and radiant. Bahá'u'lláh has even said that occupation and labor are devotion. — *'Abdu'l-Bahá*

SHARING WEALTH

Here is one of the more controversial Bahá'í social teachings. When people hear the phrase "sharing wealth" some think of charities, some think of welfare, and some think of communism. The Bahá'í approach is different from all of these. Yes, it includes some practical measures, like profit sharing, taxation proportionate to one's capacity, and public assistance for the needy, but these are secondary principles. Once again, the Bahá'í Writings call us to look at the grand picture, the universal connection between all people. They speak to our hearts in a way that makes us want to reach out and uplift our neighbor. They give us a vision of a just and compassionate future and assure us that we are moving towards that vision.

O CHILDREN OF DUST! Tell the rich of the midnight sighing of the poor, lest heedlessness lead them into the path of destruction, and deprive them of the Tree of Wealth. To give and to be generous are attributes of Mine; well is it with him that adorneth himself with My virtues. — Bahá'u'lláh

The fourth principle or teaching of Bahá'u'lláh is the readjustment and equalization of the economic standards of mankind. This deals with the question of human livelihood. It is evident that under present systems and conditions of government the poor are subject to the greatest need and distress while others more fortunate live in luxury and plenty far beyond their actual necessities. This inequality of portion and privilege is one of the deep and vital problems of human society. That there is need of an equalization and apportionment by which all may possess the comforts and privileges of life is evident. The remedy must be legislative readjustment of conditions. The rich too must be merciful to the poor, contributing from willing hearts to their needs without being forced or compelled to do so. The composure of the world will be assured by the establishment of this principle in the religious life of mankind. — 'Abdu'l-Bahá

Hearts must be so cemented together, love must become so dominant that the rich shall most willingly extend assistance to the poor and take steps to establish these economic adjustments permanently. If it is accomplished in this way, it will be most praiseworthy because then it will be for the sake of God and in the pathway of His service. For example, it will be as if the rich inhabitants of a city should say, "It is neither just nor lawful that we should possess great wealth while there is abject poverty in this community," and then willingly give their wealth to the poor, retaining only as much as will enable them to live comfortably.

Strive, therefore, to create love in the hearts in order that they may become glowing and radiant. When that love is shining, it will permeate other hearts even as this electric light illumines its surroundings. When the love of God is established, everything else will be realized. This is the true foundation of all economics. Reflect upon it. Endeavor to become the cause of the attraction of souls rather than to enforce minds. Manifest true economics to the people. Show what love is, what kindness is, what true severance is and generosity. This is the important thing for you to do. Act in accordance with the teachings of Bahá'u'lláh. — *'Abdu'l-Bahá*

O SON OF MAN! Bestow My wealth upon My poor, that in heaven thou mayest draw from stores of unfading splendor and treasures of imperishable glory. — *Bahá'u'lláh*

IMPROVING COMMUNICATION

Because abstract communication is one of the things that distinguishes us from animals, the ability to understand one another is one of the keys to seeing ourselves as one human family. Misunderstanding caused by miscommunication may not be the cause of prejudice in the world, but it certainly helps maintain it.

I read an article recently about how the media translates a common Moslem prayer as "There is no God but Allah," when in fact the prayer is: "There is no God but God." The claim that "Allah" is God infuriates many Christians who don't realize that in Arabic the word for God *is* Allah. Arabic Christians, Jews and Moslems all call God "Allah." It would be equivalent to claiming that Mexican Catholics believe in "Dios" instead God. We can see from this how a fairly minor error in translation can create incredible resentment, ill will and misunderstanding.

It is no wonder, then, that Bahá'u'lláh writes a great deal about the power of the spoken and written word, the importance of communication and the need for a universal auxiliary language.

The day is approaching when all the peoples of the world will have adopted one universal language and one common script. When this is achieved, to whatsoever city a man may journey, it shall be as if he were entering his own home. — *Bahá'u'lláh*

Bahá'u'lláh has proclaimed the adoption of a universal language. A language shall be agreed upon by which unity will be established in the world. Each person will require training in two languages: his native tongue and the universal auxiliary form of speech. This will facilitate intercommunication and dispel the misunderstandings which the barriers of language have occasioned in the world. — *'Abdu'l-Bahá*

One of the great steps towards universal peace would be the establishment of a universal language. — *'Abdu'l-Bahá*

JUSTICE

The essence of the matter is that divine justice will become manifest in human conditions and affairs, and all mankind will find comfort and enjoyment in life. — *'Abdu'l-Bahá*

The over-arching foundation of all of these social principles is justice — a justice that is born of the balance between our personal responsibility to seek out the truth for ourselves and our willingness to see, feel and understand issues from another's perspective. These two competing perspectives are served by the twin principles of independent investigation of the truth and consultation.

O SON OF SPIRIT! The best beloved of all things in My sight is Justice; turn not away therefrom if thou desirest Me, and neglect it not that I may confide in thee. By its aid thou shalt see with thine own eyes and not through the eyes of others, and shalt know of thine own knowledge and not through the knowledge of thy neighbor. Ponder this in thy heart; how it behooveth thee to be. Verily justice is My gift to thee and the sign of My loving-kindness. Set it then before thine eyes. — *Bahá'u'lláh*

Settle all things, both great and small, by consultation. Without prior consultation, take no important step in your own personal affairs. Concern yourselves with one another. Help along one another's projects and plans. Grieve over one another. Let none in the whole country go in need. Befriend one another until ye become as a single body, one and all... — *'Abdu'l-Bahá*

This is a very interesting view of justice—focusing *not* on the idea of blind justice, but rather on the need for clear-sighted justice. It speaks against the idea of precedents and for the need to look at every situation with new eyes. It is a forward-looking justice, focused on what is needed *now*—not what was decided *then*. This personal clarity is then balanced with a group decision-making process called consultation in which ego and personality is set aside in the pursuit of a higher truth.

FROM VIRTUES TO MORALS

American religions generally take two very different approaches to the question of morals. The traditional approach is to try to shove morals down people's throats through fear, guilt, shame, punishment, or a combination of all four. The more "modern" approach is to dismiss morals entirely as an antiquated system of oppression that can be dispensed with through a liberal application of the theology of forgiveness and mercy. But the Bahá'í Writings offer a third, lesser-known but very illuminating approach once we understand what morals are.

> *Divine civilization, however, so traineth every member of society that no one, with the exception of a negligible few, will undertake to commit a crime. There is thus a great difference between the prevention of crime through measures that are violent and retaliatory, and so training the people, and enlightening them, and spiritualizing them, that without any fear of punishment or vengeance to come, they will shun all criminal acts. They will, indeed, look upon the very commission of a crime as a great disgrace and in itself the harshest of punishments. They will become enamoured of human perfections, and will consecrate their lives to whatever will bring light to the world and will further those qualities which are acceptable at the Holy Threshold of God.*ʿ* — Abdu'l-Bahá*

My understanding is that morals are simply a concrete way of applying specific virtues in a particular situation. They are not arbitrary rules laid down by a killjoy God just to make life more difficult and less fun. It is hard to love a God whose main job is to keep you from enjoying yourself, and loving God is *exactly* what being moral is really all about. As I explained earlier, loving God means that we love God's virtues. When we love virtues, or, as 'Abdu'l-Bahá says we *"become enamoured of human perfections,"* we will naturally want to apply those virtues when they are appropriate. This is what most people would call "doing what is right."

If we love honesty, we will choose to tell the truth. If we love clarity and insight and the wonder of existence, we will choose

to avoid mind-numbing drugs and alcohol. If we love peace and serenity, we will naturally avoid violence. If we love justice, we will automatically want to treat people fairly.

The Bahá'í moral code is pretty similar to that of most other major religions. Gambling, begging, drugs, adultry, violence of all types, backbiting, lying, cheating, stealing, are all prohibited. It is not the morals themselves that reflect the new level of maturity that Bahá'u'lláh has told us we are entering, it is the method of *teaching* those morals that is new. Instead of just denouncing immorality, or using methods that are *"violent and retaliatory"* or based on *"fear of punishment or vengeance to come"* the Bahá'í Writings seek to establish a *"divine civilization."* They do that by focusing on the joy that comes from loving a whole host of virtues. This joy makes immoral behaviors inherently unattractive.

This joy makes immoral behaviors inherently unattractive.

the joy of chastity

If you are a parent of a teen—or perhaps a single person yourself—you may be wondering how this principle would apply to sexual morals. After all, there is no virtue so wonderful that it can compete with sex, so we *have* to use fear, punishment and guilt to keep people from having sex— don't we? Well, yes and no. Yes, we need to inspire people to reserve sexual behavior for loving, intimate, committed married relationships, but no, we don't have to use fear or guilt to do it. Our inability to name dozens of experiences and spiritual sensations that are more uplifting and enrapturing than sex tells us more about our spiritual immaturity than it says about the joys of sex. There are lots of things more fun than sex, but we have allowed our material culture to preempt our inner sources of joy.

Without an understanding of the spiritual alternatives to sexual pleasure, we are reduced to trying to scare our kids (and ourselves) away from something that everyone knows is really nice.

The problem is that fear doesn't work—and for a very good reason. When given a choice between fear and love, love always wins out. Think about it. If you were on a date, and you had the choice of thinking about

1) dying of AIDS,
2) getting pregnant,
3) getting caught and being grounded,
4) going to hell, or
5) being loved physically and emotionally,

which would YOU want to think about?

Instead of telling people that they shouldn't want love, we have to give them a vision of how much more wonderful both physical and spiritual love can be when it is combined with a few additional key virtues. Instead of demanding that they experience less fun, inspire them to expect more. Physical intimacy provides a few moments of pleasure. Sex combined with a high school crush makes you feel special for a few weeks or months. But physical intimacy combined with spiritual intimacy, respect, responsibility, integrity, commitment, purity, and reverence for the sacred miracle of procreation—these create a true magic that lasts throughout eternity. Nothing on earth compares with them. If we can get people to fall in love with this vision and these virtues, then every time there is a choice between physical love and true spiritual companionship, the more complete love will win. Sexual responsibility will not be perceived as giving something up, but rather gaining a chance at something even better.

Of course, you can't wait until your kids are sixteen to start teaching these virtues, and chastity is not the only reason to acquire them. You don't teach a child to be responsible so that they won't have sex at sixteen, you teach them responsibility so they can discover the joys of having a pet at six. As we look for ways to teach and apply virtues within our families, we begin to reflect a little bit of that divine civilization that 'Abdu'l-Bahá

talked about. Our homes can create an environment in which people appreciate responsibility, integrity and commitment, and in which life is cherished and friendships are open, honest and intimate. Only in this way will our children acquire the spiritual resources they need to make good decisions when the time comes.

following instructions vs. following examples

So what ever happened to good old fashioned obedience? Why not just force ourselves to do what God told us to do and forget about all of this subjective virtues stuff? Well, it is true, obedience is a fine virtue. Obedience—and your fear of being punished for *not* obeying—are very useful when you can't think of any other reasons for being good. But it doesn't replace the value of at least *trying* to think of some rational, emotional or spiritual reason to do the right thing. The same standard applies to moral reasoning as applies to scientific reasoning. As was quoted earlier:

"How can man believe that which he knows to be opposed to reason? Is this possible? Can the heart accept that which reason denies?"
— 'Abdu'l-Bahá

Forcing yourself (or your children) to obey without understanding does teach obedience, but it doesn't reinforce any other virtues, and may, in fact, increase resentment, anger, and even rebellion. We need to understand that the old ways of teaching morals—by manipulating people to be obedience through guilt, fear and punishment—no longer work for most people. We must use the much more difficult, but infinitely more effective source of guidance: example.

Guidance hath ever been given by words, and now it is given by deeds. Every one must show forth deeds that are pure and holy, for words are the property of all alike, whereas such deeds as these belong only to Our loved ones. Strive then with heart and soul to distinguish yourselves by your deeds.
— Bahá'u'lláh

THEOLOGICAL TEACHINGS

At the beginning of this book, I introduced some basic Bahá'í teachings that I said formed the foundation of a coherent system of beliefs. In that section I introduced some concepts like the unknowable nature of God, the common source of all religions, the role of the Prophets of God, and the difference between social and spiritual teachings. Now I would like to round out those brief explanations with some additional thoughts and some more quotations from the Bahá'í writings . .

THE NATURE OF GOD

That which we imagine, is not the Reality of God; He, the Un-knowable, the Unthinkable, is far beyond the highest conception of man. — 'Abdu'l-Bahá

understanding the trinity

Three-in-one: Father Son and Holy Spirit. No concept in Christianity has been understood less and fought over more than the Trinity. Councils have been held, churches have been divided and wars have been fought—all over a word that doesn't even appear in the Bible. Thousands, perhaps millions have died because of these disagreements, and yet today, the average Christian will tell you that they don't really understand exactly how it works. It is an article of Faith—a paradox—that most people do not even attempt to reconcile.

Bahá'u'lláh explained Christ's three-fold nature

Well, you may be surprised to hear that Bahá'ís absolutely believe in the Trinity—but not as a paradox. Bahá'u'lláh explained His three-fold nature in a way that makes such rational sense that it left me shaking my head in wonder that I hadn't figured it out before.

Briefly, imagine a beautiful, perfectly polished mirror that is turned upwards so that it reflects the light of the sun on a cloudless day. If that mirror could talk, it could say with complete honesty, "Look at me and behold the sun!" Likewise, it could say, "Look at me and see a humble mirror sitting on the ground." Finally, it would also be accurate if the mirror said, "Look and see the rays of sunlight reflect perfectly on my spotless surface."

Sun, mirror or light—Which do you see when you look at the mirror? Father, Son or Holy Spirit—which do you see when you look at Jesus the Christ? All three you say? Well that is the mystery of the Trinity.

God is like the Sun. The Holy Spirit is the Sun's Light, and Christ is a perfect mirror reflecting the Spirit of God.

Because this idea is so important to understanding both Christianity and the Bahá'í Faith, I would like to explore the metaphor more fully as I move ahead to talk about the nature of God and the role of the Prophets.

As I said before, God is beyond our ability to comprehend, but that doesn't mean that there is no relationship between God and humanity. Let's look more deeply into the analogy of the sun. The sun is visible to us, and is the source of all light and life on the planet, and yet the only direct experience we can possibly have with the sun is through its rays. The rays of light that come from the sun are just byproducts of the sun's reality. It is not a big ball of light; it is a churning mass of exploding and fusing elementary particles, heavy atoms and gravitational forces that *generate* light. If even a cupful of the essence of the sun were to fall upon the earth, it would destroy us completely.

In the same way, God, the Creator and Divine Essence, cannot come and live on earth in a human body. What *can* come and live on earth—or at least express itself on earth—is the Holy Spirit. The Holy Spirit is equivalent to the rays of light that come from the Sun. You cannot have the sun without light—or sunlight without the sun. They are inseparable. And yet, it is clear that the sun is the one generating the light—the light does not generate the sun. God is the Source, and the Holy Spirit is the blessing that gives life to the world of humanity.

Now lets consider the mirror. Since we are all "made in the image of God," we could say that we are *all* mirrors of the Holy Spirit. The problem is that we are so covered with the dirt and muck of the material world that we don't even recognize our ability to reflect. What we need is an example of a mirror that has been polished by God Himself—a perfect mirror. This mirror not only provides us with a tangible image of God that can live and breathe and love and teach right here on earth, but it also proves to us that it is possible to reflect some of God's light (the Holy Spirit) ourselves.

Now here is the big question. What if there is more than one perfect mirror? We know that there is only one God. We

What if there is more than one perfect mirror?

know that the light of the Holy Spirit shines equally on all of us. That means that every perfect mirror can honestly say "Look at Me and see the face of God." Each mirror can also say "the Father is in me." And each can honestly say "I am but a man like you—I am just a simple mirror—it is God to whom all glory is due." And here is another critical truth. Each can say "I am the same reflection that your ancestors saw a thousand years ago."

This is why Jesus could say "If you had known Moses, you would have known Me." It is why Bahá'u'lláh can claim to be the return of the Spirit of Christ—because He reflects the same Holy Spirit. This is the logic behind the Bahá'í belief in the common foundation of all major religions. It explains how Christ can both be "the only way" and also be one of many. There can be many mirrors and still be only one light.

Here is how the Bahá'í Writings explain these ideas:

prophets as perfect mirrors

To every discerning and illumined heart it is evident that God, the unknowable Essence, the divine Being, is immensely exalted beyond every human attribute, such as corporeal existence, ascent and descent, egress and regress. Far be it from His glory that human tongue should adequately recount His praise, or that human heart comprehend His fathomless mystery. He is and hath ever been veiled in the ancient eternity of His Essence, and will remain in His Reality everlastingly hidden from the sight of men....

The door of the knowledge of the Ancient of Days being thus closed in the face of all beings, the Source of infinite grace, according to His saying: "His grace hath transcended all things; My grace hath encompassed them all" hath caused those luminous Gems of Holiness [the Prophets] to appear out of the realm of the spirit, in the noble form of the human temple, and be made manifest unto all men, that they may impart unto the world the mysteries of the unchangeable Being, and tell of the subtleties of His imperishable Essence. These sanctified Mirrors, these Day-springs of ancient glory are one and all the Exponents on earth of Him Who is the central Orb of the universe, its Essence and ultimate Purpose. From Him proceed their knowledge and power; from Him is derived their sovereignty. The beauty of their countenance is but a reflection of His image, and their revelation a sign of His deathless glory. They are the Treasuries of divine knowledge, and the Repositories of celestial wisdom. Through them is transmitted a grace that is infinite, and by them is revealed the light that can never fade. — Bahá'u'lláh

Shouldst thou, however, turn thy gaze unto a Mirror, brilliant, stainless, and pure, wherein the divine Beauty is reflected, therein wilt thou find the Sun shining with Its rays, Its heat, Its disc, Its fair form all entire. For each separate entity possesseth its allotted portion of the solar light and telleth of the Sun, but that Universal Reality in all Its splendor, that stainless Mirror Whose qualities are appropriate to the qualities of the Sun revealed within It—expresseth in their entirety the attributes of the Source of Glory. And that Universal Reality is Man, the divine Being, the Essence that abideth forever....

This is the meaning of the Messiah's words, that the Father is in the Son. Dost thou not see that should a stainless mirror proclaim, 'Verily is the sun ashine within me, together with all its qualities, tokens and signs', such an utterance by such a mirror would be neither deceptive nor false?....

Such were the words uttered by Christ. On account of these words they cavilled at and assailed Him when He said unto them, 'Verily the Son is in the Father, and the Father is in the Son.' 1 John 14:11
— 'Abdu'l-Bahá

...Reflecting the same light of God

This is the changeless Faith of God, eternal in the past, eternal in the future. Let him that seeketh, attain it; and as to him that hath refused to seek it—verily, God is Self-Sufficient, above any need of His creatures. — Bahá'u'lláh

The foundation of all the divine religions is one. All are based upon reality. — 'Abdu'l-Bahá

Blessed souls whether Moses, Jesus, Zoroaster, Krishna, Buddha, Confucius, or Muhammad were the cause of the illumination of the world of humanity. How can we deny such irrefutable proof? How can we be blind to such light? How can we dispute the validity of His Holiness Christ? This is injustice. This is a denial of reality. Man must be just. We must set aside bias and prejudice. We must abandon the imitations of ancestors and forefathers. We ourselves must investigate reality and be fair in judgment. — 'Abdu'l-Bahá

Therefore, if the religions investigate reality and seek the essential truth of their own foundations, they will agree and no difference will be found. But inasmuch as religions are submerged in dogmatic imitations, forsaking the original foundations, and as imitations differ widely, therefore, the religions are divergent and antagonistic. These imitations may be likened to clouds which obscure the sunrise; but reality is the sun. If the clouds disperse, the Sun of Reality shines upon all, and no difference of vision will exist. The religions will then agree, for fundamentally they are the same. The subject is one, but predicates are many. — 'Abdu'l-Bahá

THE PURPOSE AND STATION OF THE PROPHETS

Some people feel that by referring to Jesus as a "Prophet" rather than as "God" we are trying to lower Jesus to the level of a street-corner preacher. Nothing could be further from the truth. We are holding Jesus up as the "Word of God made flesh," and we are elevating God Himself to an even higher position—one beyond our ability to comprehend. This means that all of the things we thought we knew about God actually only apply to His Prophets—those Who manifest His qualities on earth. In fact, the term Bahá'ís prefer to use is "Manifestation." "Manifest" means "apparent to the senses or the mind...to show plainly." This is what the "Manifestations of God" do for us. They make the qualities of an unknowable God apparent to humanity. But since this is a word that almost no one but Bahá'ís use, we often use the word "prophet" to refer to this very small and very special group of people. But this word is also confusing because there are so many prophets named in the Old Testament and elsewhere in religious history. Isaiah, Elijah, Ezekiel, etc. *did* tell us important things about God, but were *not* Manifestations. Bahá'ís refer to them as "lesser prophets," or "prophets not endowed with constancy." In other words, they were *in tune* with the Holy Spirit, but were not perfect, infallible reflections of the Holy Spirit. Unless otherwise noted, every reference to Prophets in this book refer to the "Greater Prophets" that Bahá'ís call Manifestations.

> *We are holding Jesus up as the "Word of God made flesh," and we are elevating God Himself to an even higher position...*

... *The Prophets and Messengers of God have been sent down for the sole purpose of guiding mankind to the straight Path of Truth. The purpose underlying Their revelation hath been to educate all men, that they may, at the hour of death, ascend, in the utmost purity and sanctity and with absolute detachment, to the throne of the Most High. The light which these souls radiate is responsible for the progress of the world and the advancement of its peoples. They are like unto leaven which leaveneth the world of being, and constitute the animating force through which the arts and wonders of the world are made manifest. Through them the clouds rain their bounty upon men, and the earth bringeth forth its fruits. All things must needs have a cause, a motive power, an animating principle. These souls and symbols of detachment have provided, and will continue to provide, the supreme moving impulse in the world of being.*

— Bahá'u'lláh

The Prophets of God should be regarded as physicians whose task is to foster the well-being of the world and its peoples, that, through the spirit of oneness, they may heal the sickness of a divided humanity. To none is given the right to question their words or disparage their conduct, for they are the only ones who can claim to have understood the patient and to have correctly diagnosed its ailments. No man, however acute his perception, can ever hope to reach the heights which the wisdom and understanding of the Divine Physician have attained. Little wonder, then, if the treatment prescribed by the physician in this day should not be found to be identical with that which he prescribed before. How could it be otherwise when the ills affecting the sufferer necessitate at every stage of his sickness a special remedy? In like manner, every time the Prophets of God have illumined the world with the resplendent radiance of the Day Star of Divine knowledge, they have invariably summoned its peoples to embrace the light of God through such means as best befitted the exigencies of the age in which they appeared. They were thus able to scatter the darkness of ignorance, and to shed upon the world the glory of their own knowledge. It is towards the inmost essence of these Prophets, therefore, that the eye of every man of discernment must be directed, inasmuch as their one and only purpose hath always been to guide the erring, and give peace to the afflicted.... — Bahá'u'lláh

Why am I going into such detail about the two kinds of prophets in this relatively short introduction to the Bahá'í teachings? For two reasons:

First, because if you think that Bahá'ís equate Jesus with Isaiah, then you would be right to argue with us. If you think we are trying to lower the station of Jesus the Christ, then you have a right to be upset. We are not. The Manifestations of God only appear once every 600-1200 years. They are the founders of the major world religions, and they lived perfect, stainless lives of loving self-sacrifice. And second, because understanding the unique station of the Prophets that we call "Manifestations" makes it easier to recognize them.

Understanding the station of the Prophets makes it easier to recognize them.

Recognizing the prophets

There are two ways to recognize a Manifestation of God—through a process of observation and through a process of elimination.

Manifestations of God reflect the Virtues of God Himself. Therefore, you should be able to observe these virtues in three overlapping spheres: Their teachings, Their lives and Their communities. In other words, you can recognize the Manifestations by the results they produced—also known as Their fruit.

Beware of false prophets, which come to you in sheep's clothing, but inwardly they are ravening wolves. Ye shall know them by their fruits. Do men gather grapes of thorns, or figs of thistles? Even so every good tree bringeth forth good fruit; but a corrupt tree bringeth forth evil fruit. A good tree cannot bring forth evil fruit, neither can a corrupt tree bring forth good fruit. Every tree that bringeth not forth good fruit is hewn down, and cast into the fire. Wherefore by their fruits ye shall know them. Mt 7:15-20

Matthew warns us not to be fooled, but Bahá'u'lláh offers an equally important warning—not to reject every potential prophet just because you don't recognize the name.

Beware lest any name debar you from Him Who is the Possessor of all names, or any word shut you out from this Remembrance of God, this Source of Wisdom amongst you. — Bahá'u'lláh

'Abdu'l-Bahá reminds us to look beyond the Prophets' names so that we come to adore the virtues that They embody.

For example, we mention Abraham and Moses. By this mention we do not mean the limitation implied in the mere names but intend the virtues which these names embody. When we say Abraham, we mean thereby a manifestation of divine guidance, a center of human virtues, a source of heavenly bestowals to mankind, a dawning point of divine inspiration and perfections. These perfections and graces are not limited to names and boundaries. When we find these virtues, qualities and attributes in any personality, we recognize the same reality shining from within and bow in acknowledgment of the Abrahamic perfections. Similarly, we acknowledge and adore the beauty of Moses. Some souls were lovers of the name Abraham, loving the lantern instead of the light, and when they saw this same light shining from another lantern, they were so attached to the former lantern that they did not recognize its later appearance and illumination. Therefore, those who were attached and held tenaciously to the name Abraham were deprived when the Abrahamic virtues reappeared in Moses. Similarly, the Jews were believers in Moses, awaiting the coming of the Messiah. The virtues and perfections of Moses became apparent in Jesus Christ most effulgently, but the Jews held to the name Moses, not adoring the virtues and perfections manifest in Him. Had they been adoring these virtues and seeking these perfections, they would assuredly have believed in Jesus Christ when the same virtues and perfections shone in Him. If we are lovers of the light, we adore it in whatever lamp it may become manifest, but if we love the lamp itself and the light is transferred to another lamp, we will neither accept nor sanction it. Therefore, we must follow and adore the virtues revealed in the Messengers of God— whether in Abraham, Moses, Jesus or other Prophets—but we must not adhere to and adore the lamp. — 'Abdu'l-Bahá '

Christ was the Prophet of the Christians, Moses of the Jews - why should not the followers of each prophet recognize and honour the other prophets also? If men could only learn the lesson of mutual tolerance, understanding, and brotherly love, the unity of the world would soon be an established fact. — 'Abdu'l-Bahá

One can also recognize a Manifestation through a process of elimination that a Christian friend from high school referred to as the "liar, lunatic or Lord" test. This test is a logical exercise based on the realization that the claim of Prophethood is an outrageous one. It is a claim that demands a response. If the claim is true, then we *must* follow His teachings, and if the claim is false, we *must not* follow them. It is also a claim that does not allow for any middle ground. Just as you can't be "a little pregnant," you can't "kind of" be a Manifestation of God. You either are or you aren't. But most important, it is a claim that no one would make lightly. If someone makes a serious claim to be a messenger of God, then he must have a very good reason. The reason, according to this test, is that he is either a liar, a lunatic or the Lord.

The claim of Prophethood is a claim that demands a response.

A liar would claim to be a Prophet of God for the same reason people lie about anything else—to gain money, power, sex or admiration and fame. Even before I heard about the Bahá'í Faith, I had figured out that if a "prophet" charged money for teaching "the truth," then he wasn't from God. If he collected expensive cars, ice cream cones, or sex slaves, then he wasn't from God. And if he slapped his name and picture on everything he could find, then he wasn't from God. Real Prophets were humble servants who sacrificed everything—money, power and their own life-blood—in order to spread the truth.

Soon after becoming a Bahá'í, I learned first-hand that there was a second kind of person who claimed prophethood. My own sister, who is schizophrenic, had a relapse, and announced to me that she was a prophet just like Bahá'u'lláh. She offered me the honor of being her first disciple, and it broke my heart. She is a good, kind and intelligent person, but it didn't take a genius to realize that the rambling, manic, disjointed, slightly paranoid "truths" she was "revealing" were not the Word of God. There are probably thousands, or even millions of people around the world who, at some point in their illnesses, believe that they are hearing guidance from God. It is heartbreaking, but it need not mislead us from our search for God. If we take even a few moments to compare their words to the words of true Prophets, we will gain absolute confidence in our ability to tell the difference.

So if we look at a self-proclaimed prophet's life and it is *not* one of self-serving greed and lust for power, and if we look at his words and they are *not* the words of a rambling psychotic, then we must concede that it is at least *possible* that he is indeed a Prophet of God.

A liar would claim to be a Prophet of God to gain money, power, or fame.

In the next section of this book, I will be outlining the history of the Bahá'í Faith. Since there is no way to squeeze over a hundred and fifty years worth of information into a few dozen pages, I will be highlighting the facts that relate to this "liar, lunatic or Lord" test. It may not be possible to prove that Bahá'u'lláh is a Manifestation of God in the next few pages, but I hope that I can at least provide some evidence that He is *not* a liar nor a lunatic. You will have to take the next step on your own.

BAHÁ'Í HISTORY

I've been a Bahá'í for a long time, but I'm afraid I've never been terribly interested in history. I read Bahá'u'lláh's writings and decided that they were from God. I didn't require any additional proofs, so I wasn't very motivated to study the details of His life.

Now, if *I* wouldn't be interested in reading a chapter on Bahá'í history, I had to ask myself why *you*, the reader, might be interested. I came up with several answers. If none of them spark your curiosity, then just skip this section.

1. *To see how the Bahá'í Faith fits into religious history in general.*
2. *To see how Bahá'í history compares with Christian history.*
3. *To see if Bahá'u'lláh received wealth or power in return for making His claim.*
4. *To see if Bahá'u'lláh was a kind, self-sacrificing person like Jesus was.*
5. *To begin to establish a personal connection with Bahá'u'lláh.*
6. *To find out how the Bahá'í Community got to the place it is today.*
7. *To get a sense of where the Bahá'í Community might be headed in the future.*

THE BIG PICTURE

In a very real sense, the Bahá'í Faith began at the very beginning of human civilization. There is only one God, so every bit of guidance that God has ever given humanity springs from the same fountain of Revelation. Bahá'ís refer to "Adam" both as a symbol of awakening human sentience, and as a symbolic name for the first Manifestation of God. Bahá'ís see a direct connection between that symbolic first Messenger and Bahá'u'lláh.

The Bahá'í Faith began at the very beginning of human civilization.

"*Contemplate with thine inward eye the chain of successive Revelations that hath linked the Manifestation of Adam with that of the Báb. I testify before God that each one of these Manifestations hath been sent down through the operation of the Divine Will and Purpose, that each hath been the bearer of a specific Message, that each hath been entrusted with a divinely revealed Book... The measure of the Revelation with which every one of them hath been identified had been definitely foreordained....*"   — *Bahá'u'lláh*

Most of the names and histories of the very early Prophets have been forgotten, but we do know a little about the Messengers of the last 6000 years. Though the details of Their lives and teachings differ—reflecting the different times and places that They lived—there are some similarities that are worth noting.

First, They showed great compassion for the oppressed and needy. Second, They had innate knowledge—being wise beyond Their years and knowledgeable beyond what Their schooling would have provided. Third, They were persecuted unfairly by the religious and political leaders of Their time. Fourth, They suffered terribly, even though They could have escaped Their suffering by recanting Their claims. And finally, They all spoke of a time in the future when They, or someone like Themselves, would return and establish peace and justice in the world.

the lens through which we see

I wish that there were some way to make a fairly long and complicated history seem easy and familiar to you, but it is difficult. The names I will use will seem strange. The places will remind you more of recent wars than holy places, and the cultural references will be distinctly "un-American." It will be difficult for you to feel comfortable with Bahá'í history from this perspective. There is, however, a *different* mysterious, ancient, Middle-Eastern religion that you probably *do* feel fairly comfortable with, and that is Christianity. If I can help you see Bahá'í history through a Christian lens, then perhaps it won't seem so strange or foreign. That is why I will be drawing parallels between significant historical elements of the life of Jesus and the history of the Bahá'í Faith. There are a lot of them.

If I can help you see Bahá'í history through a Christian lens, then perhaps it won't seem so strange or foreign.

pre-history

Before Jesus was even born, the people of Israel were expecting the arrival of the Messiah—the King of the Jews—who would sit on the throne of David, carry a sword and lead an army to deliver His people from the Roman oppressors. They had great hopes with some very specific expectations. The prophecies concerning that time were so widespread that three Zoroastrian Priests (a.k.a. the Wise Men), who were following prophecies of the Persian Prophet Zoroaster, came looking for Him. King Herod took the prophecies so seriously that he was willing to kill every child under the age of two in the city of Bethlehem in order to protect his position.

The mid 1800's was also a time of great expectation—this time for both Christians and Moslems. Christ's three promises concerning the timing of His return were about to come to pass. The Gospel had been preached in every nation, the Jews were beginning to return to Israel, and by many scholars' calculations, the "abomination of desolation" spoken of by Daniel and referred to by Christ would be fulfilled sometime around 1843 or 1844. There are several excellent books about how and why Christian prophecy points to this particular time, but this is not one of them.* Let's just say that there were as many "end of the world" preachers in 1842 as there were in 1999 before the new millennium.

The mid 1800's was a time of great expectation for both Christians and Moslems.

A particularly influential Baptist scholar named William Miller convinced many thousands of people that Christ would return either in April of 1843, or on October 22, 1844. When Christ did not appear on physical clouds in the blue sky as expected, it went down in religious history as "the Great Disappointment."

Like the Jews looking for a Warrior King, and rejecting the King of Kings, too many people were watching the sky for a miracle and not enough were searching the earth for a Messiah.

Meanwhile, in the Islamic world, they had three sets of prophecies concerning the coming of a new Prophet—those of the Old Testament, the New Testament, and their own Islamic scripture and traditions. They had several advantages over their Christian counterparts. First, they weren't looking for someone to float down from the clouds. Second, many Christian prophecies pointed to the year 1260, not the year 1844. But for Moslems that was no problem because the year 1844 *is* the year 1260 in the Islamic calendar. Plus, they had a host of traditions concerning the return of the "Twelfth Imam" that were amazingly specific.

*If this is a subject of interest to you, I recommend Thief in the Night by William Sears, or He Cometh With Clouds by Gary Matthews.

Many books have been written about Christian and Islamic prophecies, what they meant, and all the things that lead up to the final search for "The Promised One." For now, let it suffice to say that by 1844 there was an entire school in Persia (now Iran) dedicated to studying these prophetic traditions. When the leader of the school died, he told his students to quit studying and start searching. One of the students who followed these instructions was a young man named Mulla Husayn. After forty days of prayer and fasting, Mulla Husayn was moved to travel to Shiraz. At the gate of this city, he met a young merchant named Ali-Muhammad, later known as *the Báb*.

the BÁB

The Báb's station is unique in religious history, however the role He plays within the history of the Bahá'í Faith can be compared to that of John the Baptist. John taught that the Messiah was about to come and that people should prepare themselves by repenting and being baptized. He was considered a prophet by many but a devil by others. He only ate locust and honey, and had the bad habit of speaking the truth. Soon after John baptized Jesus, Herod's wife became angry with him and asked for his head on a platter.

The role the Báb plays within the history of the Bahá'í Faith can be compared to that of John the Baptist.

If you remember, the disciples later asked Jesus, (paraphrased) "how can you be the Christ when Elijah was suppose to come first, flying down from heaven in His flaming chariot to announce your coming?" To which, Jesus replied (again paraphrasing), "He did return and announce my arrival, but no one recognized Him, so they killed Him."

Like John the Baptist, the Báb's primary mission was to announce the coming of yet another Prophet. Unlike John, who would be considered a "lesser prophet," the Báb is a Manifestation of God in His own right. He founded an independent religion, revealed laws, initiated a new calendar, and, most important, reflected the light of the Holy Spirit perfectly. His life has been explored in many exciting volumes written by true historians. For the purpose of this book, however, I just want to tell you enough to give you an outline of the basic context in which Bahá'u'lláh began to teach.

In Mark, Jesus asks His disciples, *"Whom do men say that I am? And they answered, John the Baptist; but some say, Elias; and others, One of the prophets. And he saith unto them, But whom say ye that I am? And Peter answereth and saith unto him, Thou art the Christ [the anointed one]. And he charged them that they should tell no man of him." MK 8:28-30*

On May 23rd, 1844, in the city of Shiraz, Ali-Muhammad invited Mulla Husayn to his home and asked him about his quest to find the Promised One. Over the course of the evening, it became clear that Ali-Muhammad fulfilled all of the requirements of the prophecies. In addition, he began to answer questions before they were asked, and proceeded to write, with great eloquence and without pause, a treatise on a very abstract chapter in the Qur'an. By morning, Mulla Husayn was convinced that he had found the Promised One—not just because of the prophecies, but because of the kindness, wisdom, nobility, and power he had witnessed.

Ali-Muhammad called Himself "the Báb," which means "the Gate," because He considered Himself the gateway to the Prophet who was to come soon after Him.

Ali-Muhammad called Himself "the Báb," which means "the Gate," because He considered Himself the gateway to the Prophet who was to come soon after Him. He asked Mulla Husayn not

to tell anyone else about Him until eighteen individuals had independently come to recognize His station. Over the next few months, seventeen additional people did proclaim their belief in Him—some because of treatises He had published, some through dreams or visions, and one simply by seeing him walk past. All eighteen had been students at the same school of prophecy.

"The Anointed One" had His twelve, and "the Gate" had His eighteen. He sent them throughout Persia and as far away as India to publish His writings and spread His teachings. His Writings addressed many issues from abstract theology to daily prayer, but the central theme of His message was that the Promised One of All Ages was coming, and that the Day of God—a day of peace and unity—was at hand. Thousands of people embraced the new religion, from illiterate peasants to respected religious scholars. They became known as Bábís and news of their movement spread all the way to Europe.

His message was that the Promised One of All Ages was coming, and that the Day of God—a day of peace and unity—was at hand.

Here is an example of His Writing:

> By what proof hast thou embraced the Religion of Islam? Is it the Prophet on whom thou hast never set eyes? Is it the miracles which thou hast never witnessed? If thou hast accepted Islam unwittingly, wherefore hast thou done so? But if thou hast embraced the Faith by recognizing the Qur'an as the testimony, because thou hast heard the learned and the faithful express their powerlessness before it, or if thou hast, upon hearing the divine verses and by virtue of thy spontaneous love for the True Word of God, responded in a spirit of utter humility and lowliness—a spirit which is one of the mightiest signs of true love and understanding—then such proofs have been and will ever be regarded as sound.'
> — The Báb

Well, even if I hadn't told you the fate of John the Baptist, you probably could have guessed the reaction of the religious and political authorities who used religious tradition to maintain a strangle-hold on religious and political power throughout the Middle East. Most of His original eighteen followers were arrested, tortured and killed, and many others Bábís met the same fate. The Báb himself was at first placed under house arrest. Muhammad Shah, the leader of Persia, sent his most learned and trusted advisor to interview the Báb. When this advisor quickly became a devoted follower as well, the Shah became even more worried. He had the Báb imprisoned in successively more and more remote places, but nothing seemed to reduce His influence. Finally, only six years after He declared His mission, the Báb was brought to the city of Tabriz to be executed.

The story of the martyrdom of the Báb is one of the most fascinating stories in all of religious history.

Now, before I tell the rest of this story, I have to mention that Bahá'ís in general are not terribly interested in miracles. We believe that the proof of a Prophet is not in whether He can change water to wine or a river to blood, but whether He can change a human heart from hatred to love, from ignorance to wisdom, from vice to virtue. Having said that, the story of the martyrdom of the Báb is one of the most fascinating stories in all of religious history. I will tell the short version:

The Báb was to be executed, along with a young follower, by a firing squad of 750 soldiers. When the guard came for Him in the morning of July 9, 1850, He was dictating final instructions to one of His followers. He told the guard that no power on earth could harm Him until He was finished, but, of course, the guard took him away anyway. As He was being lead out, the

commander of the firing squad approached Him saying that, as a Christian, he had no desire to harm Him. The Báb assured him that if he followed his orders, God would relieve him of his dilemma.

They tied the two men face-to-face against a wall, then ten-thousand people, including some western journalists, watched as 750 old-style musket rifles were fired. It took a minute for the black smoke of that many rifles to clear, and when it did, the young man was standing against the wall—unhurt—with a scrap of shredded rope in his hands. The Báb had disappeared.

After a frantic search of the area, the guard remembered the Báb's earlier assertion. He returned to the Báb's cell and found Him finishing His dictation in a calm manner. The guard was so shaken, he resigned on the spot and left, but other guards took the Báb back to the wall to be tied up again. Meanwhile, the Christian commander refused to follow orders a second time and marched his men away.

By the time of His death, the Báb had thousands of followers throughout Persia.

The second time, the bullets of 750 Moslem soldiers found their mark, pulverizing the two bodies, but leaving the faces remarkably untouched.

Obviously, the martyrdom of Ali-Muhammad, the Báb did not succeed in destroying the religion He founded, any more than the deaths of John the Baptist and Jesus the Christ succeeded in ending Christianity. By the time of His death, the Báb had thousands of followers throughout Persia. One of the most respected of His followers was Mirza Husayn Ali, known by the Babís as Bahá'u'lláh.

BAHÁ'U'LLÁH

Unlike the Báb, who was a merchant, Mirza Husayn Ali was born into one of the leading noble families of Iran. His father was an important minister in the court of the Shah. He had great wealth, a luxurious home, private gardens, land, servants, a beautiful wife, several children, and the respect of most of the people of the city of Tehran. Mirza Husayn Ali was known for His unusual wisdom. Like Jesus who discussed theology with the rabbis when just a child, Mirza Husayn Ali argued a property case in court on behalf of His father when He was only seven—and won. When His father died, He was offered his position in the court, but declined. Instead, He and His wife dedicated themselves to serving the people of their community, earning the names "Father and Mother of the Poor."

In short, Mirza Husayn Ali had absolutely nothing to gain—and a great deal to lose—when He decided to join the unpopular new Babí religion and become one of its leading defenders. Like Simon, whom Jesus renamed Peter, the Rock, and Saul who called himself Paul, many

Mirza Husayn Ali had absolutely nothing to gain— and a great deal to lose—when He decided to join the unpopular new Babí religion

of the Babís took new names expressing their love for God. Mirza Husayn Ali took the name Bahá'u'lláh, which means "Glory of God."

When the Báb was arrested in 1846, Bahá'u'lláh could have quietly disavowed His relationship with the Babís and returned to His life of wealth and power, but instead, He used His influence to assist the Babí community. When He was Himself arrested in 1847, He could have recanted His faith and gone home safely. But He didn't. When the authorities started torturing and killing Babís; when He was re-arrested and beaten; when the

Báb Himself was martyred; when large-scale massacres began; these would all have been logical times for a power-hungry or manipulative liar to see the writing on the wall and abandon the Babí Community and the teachings of the Báb. But He didn't. He suffered arrest, imprisonment, torture and banishment solely for the sake of God.

This might be a good place to remind you of why Jesus *was arrested.* With all of this talk about multiple arrests, it might be a good place to remind you of why *Jesus* was arrested. No one said, "Oh, here is the Son of God. I think I'll kill Him." Nor did Jesus say, "Hey Herod, I'm the rightful King of the Jews. Please step down and let me take over." Jesus simply offered a new and powerful vision of the world. "New and powerful" equals "dangerous" in the minds of those who cling to traditional sources of power. Likewise, the Báb and Bahá'u'lláh did not advocate the violent overthrow of the government. They did, however, say that we were mature enough to study sacred scripture without the need for clergy, promoted the equality of women, upheld the value of science and reason, and said that all religions are equal. You can imagine how the people in power at the time perceived these teachings. You can also see why thousands of people, including Bahá'u'lláh, were willing to risk their lives to promote them. This is where the battle between Islamic Fundamentalism and modernism began, and, as you know, it is still raging.

So, by 1852, with the Báb dead and the Shah authorizing the arrest and murder of hundreds of Babís, it is disappointing, but not surprising, that two young Bábís, "crazed with grief" tried to shoot the Shah. The attempt was poorly planned and the pistol was too small to do any harm, yet the incident was all that was needed to justify accusations of a conspiracy. Within days, most of the surviving Babí leaders had been killed, and an organized campaign to wipe out the entire community was underway. Over the course of the next few decades, over twenty thousand Babís would be systematically hunted down, tortured and killed.

It was at this dark and dangerous juncture that Bahá'u'lláh was arrested again and placed in an underground prison so foul that it almost defies the imagination. Three stories underground, it had originally served as a reservoir for the public baths. It received no daylight and little fresh air, but had plenty of seeping water, human waste, rats, roaches, and murderous company. Of the 150 men who were chained ankle-to-ankle down the dark chamber, only a few dozen were fellow Babís. The rest were murderers, highwaymen and thieves. Bahá'u'lláh was given the 'honor' of wearing one of the two sets of chains that were so heavy that they were given names by the prisoners. The heavier of the two weighed almost as much as Bahá'u'lláh himself, and had to be supported by a wooden fork. They dug into His flesh so deeply that He wore the scars his entire life. He could neither lie down nor stand erect, and if any of the men wanted to move more than a few inches, every other man would have to shift position as well.

Bahá'u'lláh was arrested again and placed in an underground prison so foul that it almost defies the imagination.

In addition to the oppressive darkness, smell, chains and company, the Babís also bore the weight of knowing that almost every day one of them would be lead out of the prison to face execution. The first three days, Bahá'u'lláh was given no food, and when food finally was provided, it was poisoned. He was weakened, but did not die. Instead, He taught His fellow prisoners to sing songs based on the prayers of the Báb, and they would chant them both day and night. The irony of this was that the underground chambers were linked to sewer tunnels that ran throughout the city, so the sound of their chanting could be heard all the way to the palace of the Shah.

I would like to step back from this scene for a moment and try to put it into perspective. I am writing these words on March 3rd 2004. It is the second day of the Bahá'í Fast—a time in the Bahá'í calendar similar to Lent or the Islamic Fast of Ramadan. It is an opportunity to voluntarily share in just a whisper of sacrifice. I will avoid food and drink *during daylight hours* for nineteen days. It will give me headaches and make me grumpy, but that is about the worst of my suffering. Meanwhile, in our local movie theater, *The Passion of the Christ* is playing to record crowds. To witness even a movie version of the suffering, torture, and brutal murder of Christ leaves audience members stunned, in tears, unable to speak, unable to sleep peacefully and deeply moved by the evidence of His love for all of us. And yet, Christ's suffering was mercifully short—only some twelve hours from arrest to death.

Bahá'u'lláh had to wear 110 pound chains around his neck for months at a time. Bahá'u'lláh, Who had lived a life of wealth and comfort, Who had a wife and children whom He loved and worried about, Who had done nothing wrong except to speak the truth, was cast into this foul prison—not for 12 hours, but for almost 3,000 hours—approximately 120 days. We weep over the image of Jesus carrying a heavy wooden cross through the streets of Jerusalem, but Bahá'u'lláh had to wear 110 pound chains around his neck for months at a time. I can barely drag an 80 pound bag of concrete from my car to the porch. How did He survive it? Can you imagine not being able to see the sunshine, not being able to breathe clean air, worrying about your wife and children, and not knowing if you were to be the next one led out to face the executioner? I can't. I might last a few days, but four months would have been impossible. He suffered under conditions that would have broken both the body and the spirit of any human I know, and yet He emerged spiritually stronger and more vibrant than He went in. In fact, He left the prison quite literally, a man with a mission.

As you know, before Jesus began His mission, He did two things. First, He went to John the Baptist and received the blessing of the Holy Spirit. Mark describes it this way: *And it came to pass in those days, that Jesus came from Nazareth of Galilee, and was baptized of John in Jordan. And straightway coming up out of the water, he saw the heavens opened, and the Spirit like a dove descending upon him: And there came a voice from heaven, saying, Thou art my beloved Son, in whom I am well pleased. And immediately the spirit driveth him into the wilderness. MK 1:9-12*

In the wilderness, Jesus prepared for His mission by fasting for forty days. He was tested to see if He was willing to endure suffering even when He had the power to avoid it. Even though He had always been the Christ, His *ministry* did not begin until He received His revelation from the Holy Spirit, and was tested through suffering.

He was tested to see if He was willing to endure suffering even when He had the power to avoid it.

Likewise, Bahá'u'lláh was prepared for His mission by his days in the prison of Tehran. It was in the midst of this suffering that He received His Revelation, referred to by Him symbolically as both a river of power pouring over Him and as a message delivered by a holy "maiden of heaven." Here is how He describes the experience:

'During the days I lay in the prison of Tihran, though the galling weight of the chains and the stench-filled air allowed Me but little sleep, still in those infrequent moments of slumber I felt as if something flowed from the crown of My head over My breast, even as a mighty torrent that precipitateth itself upon the earth from the summit of a lofty mountain. Every limb of My body would, as a result, be set afire. At such moments My tongue recited what no man could bear to hear.'

'One night, in a dream, these exalted words were heard on every side: "Verily, We shall render Thee victorious by Thyself and by Thy pen. Grieve Thou not for that which hath befallen Thee, neither be Thou afraid, for Thou art in safety. Ere long will God raise up the treasures of the earth - men who will aid Thee through Thyself and through Thy Name, wherewith God hath revived the hearts of such as have recognized Him." — Bahá'u'lláh

'While engulfed in tribulations I heard a most wondrous, a most sweet voice, calling above My head. Turning My face, I beheld a Maiden - the embodiment of the remembrance of the name of My Lord - suspended in the air before Me. So rejoiced was she in her very soul that her countenance shone with the ornament of the good-pleasure of God, and her cheeks glowed with the brightness of the All-Merciful. Betwixt earth and heaven she was raising a call which captivated the hearts and minds of men. She was imparting to both My inward and outer being tidings which rejoiced My soul, and the souls of God's honored servants. Pointing with her finger unto My head, she addressed all who are in heaven and all who are on earth, saying: "By God! This is the Best-Beloved of the worlds, and yet ye comprehend not. This is the Beauty of God amongst you, and the power of His sovereignty within you, could ye but understand. This is the Mystery of God and His Treasure, the Cause of God and His glory unto all who are in the kingdoms of Revelation and of creation, if ye be of them that perceive."' — Bahá'u'lláh

Moses received His revelation from a burning bush; Jesus from a talking dove. Buddha received enlightenment while sitting under a tree by a river...

This concept of "receiving One's Mission" is a difficult one. To be honest, you could use the quotations above as proof that Bahá'u'lláh was, indeed, delusional rather than a Prophet. But to do so would ignore the history of religion from the beginning of time. Moses received His revelation from a burning bush; Jesus from a talking dove. Buddha received enlightenment while sitting under a tree by a river, and Mohammed was called by the Angel Gabriel.

Each of these men lived moderately normal lives until they were awakened, enlightened or called upon by God to take their positions as Divine Teachers of humanity. If we wish, we can assume that the bush, dove, maiden, river, and angel represent spiritual realities, not physical ones. What they looked like is unimportant. How the Prophets respond to the call *is* important.

Because He had been supported by the power of the Holy Spirit, Bahá'u'lláh left the prison, not the broken, humble man they expected. Instead He was invested with even more power and authority than before.

Bahá'u'lláh left the prison invested with even more power and authority than before.

Still dressed in the torn and dirty clothes He had worn in prison, He was called before the court of the Grand Vizir.

"Had you chosen to take my advice, and had you dissociated yourself from the Faith of the Siyyid-i-Bab," said the Grand Vizir, *"you would never have suffered the pains and indignities that have been heaped upon you."*

"Had you, in your turn, followed My counsels," Bahá'u'lláh responded, *"the affairs of the government would not have reached so critical a stage."*
— Shoghi Effendi

From this brief exchange it is clear that Bahá'u'lláh could have avoided persecution and could still, probably, lessen future punishments by renouncing the Bábí cause. It is also clear that He has no intention of doing so. As a consequence, He was given one month to leave the country of Persian and never return. This was just the beginning of forty years of banishment, exile and imprisonment.

By the time Bahá'u'lláh was released from prison, all of his property and wealth had been confiscated. He had nothing. His wife, Navvab, had managed to rescue some of their clothing, and she sold the gold and silver buttons from her dresses to pay for the supplies needed for the journey to Baghdad, Iraq.

The story of Bahá'u'lláh's imprisonment should have given you some indication of His willingness to suffer for the Cause of God so I won't go into too many details concerning the midwinter trip over the mountains on mules with two small children and a wife who was pregnant while He Himself was still recovering from His ordeal. Let me move on, instead, to signs of the more charismatic aspects of Bahá'u'lláh's character—His ability to educate and inspire the people who came in contact with Him.

Bahá'u'lláh entered Baghdad an exiled ex-prisoner with no rank and no money.

Bahá'u'lláh entered Baghdad an exiled ex-prisoner—an enemy of the neighboring country with no rank, no money and no friends except for the small band of Bábí outcasts who had followed Him west. He did not announce Himself to be the new Messiah. He did not hold large gatherings or make appeals for followers. He simply worked, wrote, and spoke with people about the teachings of the Báb. Three of His most important books were written during this time—*The Book of Certitude*, which is about the progressive nature of religion; *The Seven Valleys* which is a mystical exploration of the path towards God; and *The Hidden Words*, which is a collection of meditations and spiritual guidance (and which I have quoted extensively in this book). During this time He simply filled the Bábí community with so much love, support and wisdom that it spilled out into the greater city of Baghdad and His influence began to grow.

Within ten short years, Bahá'u'lláh's influence was being felt back across the border into Persia—which made the Shah nervous again. He pressured the Sultan of the Ottoman Empire to transfer Bahá'u'lláh to a city farther away from Iran. But the Governor of Baghdad had come to love and respect Bahá'u'lláh so much that he ignored the Sultan's first five orders of banishment before he finally gave in and told Bahá'u'lláh that He was being exiled to Constantinople (now Istanbul).

To get an idea of how the people of Baghdad felt about Bahá'u'lláh, picture the stories you have heard about Palm Sunday, when Jesus rode into Jerusalem. News of His departure quickly spread throughout the city and to neighboring towns. So many people poured into the streets to try to see Bahá'u'lláh one last time and wish Him well, that Bahá'u'lláh set up a tent in a garden across the river from His home so that He could receive them all. Hundreds of people lined the streets to catch a glimpse of Him, to touch Him, to hear Him speak, and to express their love, respect and grief at His departure.

It was at this time, April 1863, in the garden that He named Ridvan, or Paradise, that He told a few of His closest family and friends that He was, indeed, the Promised One. Most had already guessed.

Ten years later, hundreds of people lined the streets to touch Him, to hear Him speak, and to express their love, respect and grief at His departure.

Once in Constantinople, the authorities only allowed Bahá'u'lláh to stay for four months before they decided to send Him even farther away—all the way to Adrianople, which is now called Edirne. If you look at a map, it is almost funny to think that the government of Persia (now Iran) felt compelled to push one innocent religious leader to the far, far, *far* side of what is now Turkey in order to feel safe. What they obviously hadn't taken into consideration was that by moving Him away from His enemies in the Middle East, they were actually bringing Him closer to a potential audience for His teachings in the more progressive countries of Europe. Adrianople is just across the Turkish border with Greece.

Bahá'u'lláh took this opportunity to publicly announce His mission and His station as a Prophet of God. He wrote letters to many of the religious and political leaders of Europe, asking them to consider His claim and to investigate the reasons for His continued exile.

I've already talked about how religious and political leaders normally respond to claims of prophethood, but this time they weren't the only ones upset by Bahá'u'lláh's claim. Bahá'u'lláh's half brother, Mirza Yahya, saw himself as the leader of the Bábí community and was so jealous that he made a counter-claim to be the true promised one. Just as it was one of Jesus's favorite disciples who betrayed Him, it was Bahá'u'lláh's own half-brother who fought to take control of the Bábí community. When the Bábís chose Bahá'u'lláh instead, Mriza Yahya spread rumors, plotted with the government, and eventually even succeeded in poisoning Bahá'u'lláh. Bahá'u'lláh survived the poisoning, but it weakened Him so much that His hand shook whenever He tried to write for the rest of His life. Interestingly, it was this shaky writing style that made Bahá'u'lláh's handwriting impossible to forge. This would become important later, when Bahá'u'lláh's Will was challenged.

When the light is brightest, then the shadows become most distinct.

I hope that someday a writer who is more gifted than I am will write the Shakespearian version of this history, because it is so full of mystery and intrigue and sacrifice and betrayal that it deserves a richer telling. And isn't this the reality of spiritual history? When the light is brightest, then the shadows become most distinct. Christ was betrayed by Judas and denied by Peter. They played important roles in the spiritual drama. Likewise, the tensions within the Bábí community do not prove that it was fundamentally flawed. Instead they demonstrate the grand epic nature of the struggles that the individuals within that community had to resolve.

Adrianople was a time of transition and transformation. Once again, Bahá'u'lláh became a respected and revered figure in the city, but a split developed between the Bábís who followed Bahá'u'lláh and the few who followed His half-brother. Those who followed Bahá'u'lláh began to call themselves Bahá'ís. Mirza Yahya spread rumors in hopes of having Bahá'u'lláh put in prison again, but his plan backfired. When, after five years, the Turkish authorities decided that Adrianople was not a smart idea after all, they decided to exile both Bábí leaders to different places. The Governor of the city defended Bahá'u'lláh against the false accusations and tried to prevent His further banishment, but to no avail. One morning His family awoke to find their house surrounded by soldiers. No one knew where they were being taken next.

The song, "Rock of Ages" is about Mt. Carmel, which is across the bay from the prison of Akka.

You've heard the song "Rock of Ages, cleft for Me, Let me hide myself in thee?" Well that song is about Mt. Carmel. Many Christians believe that this "rock" that overlooks the bay of Haifa is where Christ will first appear when He returns in the clouds. There is an entire community of people, called the German Templar Colony, who came to live in the shadow of the mountain in hopes of meeting Jesus when He returned. Well, across the bay from this mountain is a prison city called Akka. Because it is on the far east end of the Mediterranean Sea, it was strategically important, but it also collected all of the scum and debris that the wind and currents deposited. The story goes that a bird flying over the city would drop dead from the stench. This is where they brought Bahá'u'lláh, His family and followers.

This time, however, they did not simply exile Him to a new city. They told the people of the city that the Bahá'ís were enemies of Islam and that they should avoid all contact with them. Then they threw the entire group into prison, isolating Bahá'u'lláh in one cell by Himself, and cramming dozens of people into each of the remaining rooms. Many died, including one of Bahá'u'lláh's sons, before conditions began to improve. Of this time, Bahá'u'lláh wrote:

The Ancient Beauty hath consented to be bound with chains that mankind may be released from its bondage, and hath accepted to be made a prisoner within this most mighty Stronghold that the whole world may attain unto true liberty. He hath drained to its dregs the cup of sorrow, that all the peoples of the earth may attain unto abiding joy, and be filled with gladness. This is of the mercy of your Lord, the Compassionate, the Most Merciful. We have accepted to be abased, O believers in the Unity of God, that ye may be exalted, and have suffered manifold afflictions, that ye might prosper and flourish. He Who hath come to build anew the whole world, behold, how they that have joined partners with God have forced Him to dwell within the most desolate of cities!   — *Bahá'u'lláh*

Eventually, the Turkish army needed the prison, and the Bahá'ís were allowed to move into a house in town where Bahá'u'lláh remained under house arrest. Once the Bahá'ís gained some freedom of movement, their positive influence began to have an effect.

The governor of the prison sent his own son to the Bahá'ís to be educated and came to have great respect for Bahá'u'lláh. He asked Bahá'u'lláh if there was any service he could provide. Bahá'u'lláh answered that the town aqueduct, which had been unusable for thirty years, should be repaired. This improved the quality of life for everyone in the city. Though Bahá'u'lláh was technically under house arrest, the prison governor eventually convinced Him that He could just as easily be under house arrest in a home in the country. After nine years within the prison city walls, Bahá'u'lláh finally was allowed to walk in a garden and feel the grass beneath His feet. As restrictions were relaxed, He was even allowed to take the short trip to Haifa and pitch His tent on the side of Mt. Carmel. It was during one of these trips that He pointed out the places on the side of the mountain where the Shrine of the Báb and the future Bahá'í Administrative Offices were to be built.

Two years later, the owner of a new mansion fled a cholera epidemic and sold his property to the Bahá'ís at a very low price. It was in this home that Bahá'u'lláh lived the last thirteen years of His life—technically still a prisoner, but respected throughout the Middle East and even parts of Europe for His character and wisdom.

This, then, in brief, is the life of Bahá'u'lláh. For those of you who like history, the bibliography lists several longer histories that can fill in some of the details I've left out. What I hope is that I've given you enough of a sense of Bahá'u'lláh's sincerity, character and power that you can rule out the possibility that He was a liar or a lunatic.

During the forty years of His ministry—from His imprisonment in 1852 to his passing in 1892—Bahá'u'lláh spoke with thousands of people and wrote countless volumes. Though He was unknown in America until after His death, in Europe, leading thinkers and philosophers were familiar with Him. Leo Tolstoy, for example, said : "The teachings of the Bábís which come to us out of Islam have through Bahá'u'lláh's teachings been gradually developed and now present us with the highest and purest form of religious teaching."

In the years since His passing, His influence has spread to every corner of the globe and has inspired many millions of people. This means, of course, that Bahá'í history did not end in 1892.

Now, Bahá'ís do not make any claims that Bahá'u'lláh was physically resurrected. That would be inconsistent with our belief in a spiritual rather than a physical afterlife. Bahá'u'lláh's soul continues to exist on a spiritual plane, as does the soul of every Prophet, and indeed, every human who is animated by the love of God. What Bahá'u'lláh *did* do, was to appoint His eldest son, 'Abdu'l-Bahá, as His successor and the authorized interpreter and expounder of the Bahá'í teachings. The nature and scope of the authority He bestowed on 'Abdu'l-Bahá was spelled

out in great detail in His Will and Testament—which was written in His own distinctively shaky handwriting. There was, therefore, no excuse for anyone to try to wrestle control of the Bahá'í Community or its properties away from 'Abdu'l-Bahá, or to try to put their own spin on Bahá'u'lláh's teachings. Of course, that didn't stop several power-hungry relatives from trying.

So, who was 'Abdu'l-Bahá ? First of all, unlike the Báb and Bahá'u'lláh, 'Abdu'l-Bahá was *not* a Manifestation of God. He was an ordinary human—except for the fact that Bahá'u'lláh said that he was a perfect example of what a human should be, and that he was under the care, protection and unerring guidance of Bahá'u'lláh Himself. If the words "perfect" and "unerring" make you a little uncomfortable, that is OK. They sounded a little extreme to me at first as well. But let me say this: after thirty years of reading the Bahá'í Writings and saying Bahá'í Prayers written by both Bahá'u'lláh and 'Abdu'l-Bahá, I feel as close or even closer to 'Abdu'l-Bahá than I do to Bahá'u'lláh. This is my own personal response, but I will try to explain my feelings.

The way I see it, Bahá'u'lláh speaks to us as the Mouthpiece of God. 'Abdu'l-Bahá speaks to us as a human who has spent his entire lifetime looking at a perfect reflection of God. Bahá'u'lláh's Writings are lofty, mystical and powerful. 'Abdu'l-Bahá's writings are full of love and enthusiasm and hope. Bahá'u'lláh releases the creative, generative power of God. 'Abdu'l-Bahá shows us how to become receptive to it. The "Glory of the Father" would leave me too full of awe if it were not mediated by the humanity of 'Abdu'l-Bahá.

In short, I could not feel at home in the Bahá'í Faith if I didn't have access to both of these perspectives. I can't separate the two. Once I fell in love with the teachings of Bahá'u'lláh, it took very little effort to place my whole confidence in the explanations and guidance given by His chosen successor.

'Abdu'l-Bahá

'Abdu'l-Bahá was born Abbas Effendi on May 23rd 1844. If that date seems to ring a bell with you, it is because it is the exact same date on which the Báb announced His station to Mulla Husayn. He was nine years old when his Father was thrown into prison and his family was forced into hiding. A few months later, when his Father was released, he was the first to recognize the change that had taken place and believe in his Father's new station, though he told no one.

As a young man, 'Abdu'l-Bahá gradually took over the day-to-day administration of his Father's affairs. Bahá'u'lláh called him "the Master," though he preferred the title 'Abdu'l-Bahá, which means "Servant of Bahá." He was al-

'Abdu'l-Bahá was selfless, wise, hard working and kind, full of humor and generosity.

lowed much greater freedom of movement than his Father, and so he became the public face of the Bahá'í Community. He was selfless, wise, hard working and kind, full of humor and generosity. He cared for the sick, helped the poor and organized community service projects. Because he was not under house arrest for as many years as Bahá'u'lláh, we actually have many more stories and anecdotes about his interactions with the people of Akka and Haifa. We also have very detailed accounts of his visits to Europe and America.

For the sake of brevity, I will skip over the stories about jealous family members, renewed imprisonment, commissions of inquiry, and a pending execution reversed by the Young Turk revolution at the last moment. Lets just say that in spite of many difficulties, 'Abdu'l-Bahá succeeded in spreading Bahá'í teachings even farther than before, developing a regular correspondence with Bahá'í communities in Europe and America. By 1898 he received his first visitors—what Bahá'ís call pilgrims—

from the United States. Within a few more years, the American community numbered in the thousands and stretched from coast to coast. In 1911, having been officially freed in 1907, he set out for a journey to Europe and America.

What an amazing trip. Consider the fact that he was now sixty-eight years old. He had been a prisoner since the age of nine, and had never attended any school. Aside from a short trip to Egypt, he had never traveled as a free man and had never experienced any culture outside of the Middle East. He had no experience at public speaking, spoke almost no English, and wore a robe and a turban. Who would imagine that he would be received with such enthusiasm everywhere he went? He drew large crowds wherever he spoke, including churches and cathedrals. He also had private conversations with leading philanthropists, scientists and politicians, including Alexander Graham Bell, explorer Admiral Peary, members of Congress, and Theodore Roosevelt.

Unlike many of the spiritual leaders of today, he did not ask for any money for his trip.

Unlike many of the spiritual leaders of today, he did not ask for any money for his trip. He declined to accept free tickets for the maiden voyage of the Titanic (yes, *that* Titanic) and paid for his own assorted accommodations. He even distributed a quarter to every homeless man who attended his talk at the bowery mission in New York. Wherever he went, he only asked two things of the Bahá'ís. First, he asked them to love one another—no matter how hard it might seem. Second, he asked the Bahá'ís (and only the Bahá'ís*) to raise money for a House of Worship to be built north of Chicago and which would be open to members of all religions. He laid the cornerstone of that House of Worship himself.

*Bahá'ís can't accept money from any outside sources.

The record of this 239-day trip is contained in dozens of histories as well as autobiographies from Bahá'ís who witnessed his perfect example personally. The hundreds of talks he gave are recorded in a volume called *The Promulgation of Universal Peace*—which gives you an idea of the major theme of many of his presentations. He spoke to Jews about the station of Christ and Christians about the station of Muhammad. He spoke to the wealthy about the importance of philanthropy and to the poor about God's deep love for them. Everywhere he went, he encour-

The hundreds of talks he gave in America are recorded in a volume called The Promulgation of Universal Peace.

aged love, understanding and unity. His visit galvanized the American Bahá'í Community and made it one of the most pro-active and self-sacrificing spiritual movements in the world.

On his return, he continued to correspond with Bahá'ís around the world right up until the time of his passing in 1921. Though he is not considered a Prophet, his unique station as perfect example and authorized translator means that his books, letters, and, to a lesser degree, his talks, are considered a part of the Bahá'í Sacred Writings. Many of them have been quoted earlier in this book. As you read them I'm sure you will see why they hold such a special place in the hearts of Bahá'ís every-where.

FROM EASTERN PHENOMENON TO GLOBAL RELIGION

The loss of 'Abdu'l-Bahá was a great blow to the Community, but it was, perhaps felt most deeply by a 24 year-old grandson named Shoghi Effendi, who was studying English at Oxford University when he received the news. Upon his return to Haifa, he learned that 'Abdu'l-Bahá had named him as his successor and given him the title "The Guardian of the Cause" in his Will and Testament. The role and station of the Guardian, as described by 'Abdu'l-Bahá, was a very interesting one. On one hand, he was neither a Prophet, nor a perfect human. On the other hand, in order to keep the Community from splitting into pieces, he was given absolute authority to guide the Faith and to interpret and apply its laws.

'Abdu'l-Bahá named Shoghi Effendi as his successor

Shoghi Effendi was the perfect instrument for holding the Bahá'í Community together during a period of great transition. With his Oxford training and impressive command of the English language, it was as though he had one foot in the mystical world of the East, and the other in the practical world of the West. In some ways, he was similar to Paul, who helped put the teachings of Christ into a language and context that appealed to Romans rather than just Jews, and helped Christianity spread beyond Israel. His major accomplishments include the translation of significant portions of Bahá'u'lláh's and 'Abdu'l-Bahá 's writing into English, the organization and clarification of universal Bahá'í administrative principles, the gradual implementation of Bahá'í laws in western Bahá'í communities, the acquisition and expansion of Bahá'í properties in Haifa and Akka, the protection of the Faith from attacks, and the vast geographic spread of the teachings through organized campaigns of travel and relocation.

112

Through his vision, determination, support, enthusiasm, organization and inspiration, he raised the number of countries with Bahá'í communities from 35 to over 200, and expanded the number of languages in which writings were translated from 41 to 230. By the time of his passing in 1957, the Bahá'í Faith was well on its way to being recognized as a major world religion.

In 1953 he had launched a ten-year global campaign that was to culminate in the democratic election of the first international Bahá'í council, called the Universal House of Justice. When he passed away unexpectedly without appointing a successor or leaving a will, Bahá'ís weren't sure what to do. There were some, I'm afraid, who wanted to appoint *themselves* the new guardian, while others wanted to push the election forward by five years. But the majority of the Bahá'í Community was committed to following the original timetable, and in April of 1963, the first Universal House of Justice was elected on the 100th anniversary of Bahá'u'lláh's declaration of His Mission in the garden of Ridvan outside of Baghdad.

Since then, the Bahá'í Community has continued to grow. The Encyclopedia Brittanica lists it as the most geographically wide-spread religion on earth after Christianity, representing over 2,100 ethnic, racial, and tribal groups and number some five million believers. There are Bahá'ís in over 230 countries and 110,000 localities. But those are just numbers. What those numbers represent is a community that may well be the most *diverse and widespread* of any organized body of people on earth. More importantly, it may be the most "diverse and widespread" community on earth that is both spiritually and materially unified. Most *amazingly* it is definitely the most "diverse and widespread" community whose activities are governed by a body that is *democratically elected* by a tiered system that reaches right down into the grass-root grass-covered huts and homes of our global village. Imagine that.

✳ MY BAHÁ'Í FAITH
BAHÁ'Í COMMUNITY

When a villager living in a hut in New Zealand votes for a delegate from that local area, he or she is participating at the same level and in the same process as I do when I vote for my delegate from southern Indiana. Those votes eventually help determine who is elected to serve on the single international governing body of the Bahá'í Community. But let's back up a bit and start at the local level.

Bahá'ís have no clergy, but that *doesn't* mean they believe in anarchy. Communities are organized around elected councils called Local Spiritual Assemblies. This is a body of nine individuals who are elected by secret ballot without nominations and without campaigning from all of the eligible adult members of the local community. In practice, what this means is that every adult in the community gets together on April 20th and each writes down the names of the nine people he or she thinks would do the best job of serving the community. That's it. The nine with the most names are given the responsibility of guiding the community for that year.

Those nine individuals have no power, privilege or perks in connection with their service on the Assembly. They are obligated to use a process called *consultation* to arrive at decisions. This means they are supposed to set aside ego and ownership of ideas and work as a loving, listening, well-intentioned group that turns to God for guidance and places principles before personality.

Bahá'ís like to say that it is a perfect system being operated by imperfect people. Democracy is always a little "messy" because it involves so many diverse people and opinions, but it is the best system for a maturing society. The Bahá'í system of democracy invites an even wider range of diverse opinions, so it does not always operate smoothly. But as civilization moves towards adulthood, it will be the best possible system for utilizing our increased capacity and maturity.

In addition to Local Spiritual Assemblies, there are Regional Councils, National Spiritual Assemblies and the Universal House of Justice. Each of these is elected in the same way through a tiered system of representatives. In the U.S. for example, five Regional Councils are elected by the members of all of the local Assemblies in their area. National Assemblies are elected by delegates who are themselves elected by all the eligible adults in a given area. Every five years, the members of National Assemblies elect the Universal House of Justice. This council oversees the activities of Bahá'í communities around the world, and operates out of the Bahá'í World Center in Haifa Israel.

But the elected councils are only one-half of the Bahá'í structure. We also have what are called *the Institutions of the Learned*. These are individuals who are appointed to inspire, encourage and guide the Community and individuals within it. While the elected councils have legislative powers but can only operate as a body, the "learned" operate as individuals, but have absolutely no power except the power of wisdom and example. Like the elected bodies, the Institution of the Learned operates on the international, national, regional and local levels. The interaction between individuals and councils, between the learned and the elected, between inspirers and organizers, between local, national and international arms, all create a dynamic flow of ideas, creativity and vision that keeps the Community adaptable and adapting.

All of these individuals and institutions also interact with the world at large. Bahá'ís have an office at the United Nations where we have consultative status as a Non-Governmental Organization. On the local level, Bahá'ís work with many like-minded organizations. For example, in my local community, I served on the city's Martin Luther King Commission, Judy meets with Interfaith Prayers for Peace, Dan is involved with Youth Workshop and a "United City" anti-hate group, and Naomi has created an organization to host children's diversity festivals.

✳ MY BAHÁ'Í FAITH
A WORK IN PROGRESS

My description of the Bahá'í community might lead you to believe that the Bahá'í Faith is a finished product—something I can draw a box around and write a book about saying "here is my Bahá'í Faith." But it isn't and I can't. The process of revelation may have come to an end, but the process of *application* has only just begun. The Bahá'í Community is very much a work in progress. It is an evolving, organic, living entity. As one of my favorite Bahá'í speakers explained, it is a workshop, not a showcase. The goal of this workshop, it is important to remember, is the reorganization of the entire human race and the establishment of peace and unity within a spiritualized world culture. This is a more ambitious project than any other religion in history has been in a position to attempt.

The Bahá'í Community is a workshop, not a showcase.

If you have ever been in a workshop, then you know that they are not very pretty places. They are often dirty, chaotic, loud, and even disorganized at times. Materials are moved from here to there and back again. Molds and scaffolding are put together then taken apart again. Sometimes the final product is impossible to visualize from the pieces and parts that compose it. But there is something else that is true about a workshop. It is a creative place full of energy, enthusiasm and inspiration. People working together for a common, constructive goal learn how to communicate, cooperate and collaborate in ways that others never have to.

At the risk of scaring people away, anyone interested in actually participating in Bahá'í activities needs to know that this is not a religion for people who want to sit in the back row and watch the same liturgy for the next twenty years. It is a participatory religion—a religion where you only benefit from it if you are willing to roll up your shirtsleeves and start hammering—even if tomorrow you find you have to pull out all the nails and start again. Lots of people working side by side means lots of changes, lots of mistakes, lots of backtracking, lots of compromises, lots of progress, lots of fun, lots of pain, lots of growth. I won't pretend that it is easy. It isn't. In fact I wrote an entire book called *Falling Into Grace* about the 'Trials and Triumphs of Becoming a Bahá'í." But the work we are doing is very important. It is also rewarding. So I encourage you to consider it.

All of this talk about workshops and change is simply to say that it is impossible for me to tell you what any particular part of the Bahá'í Community will look like or act like at any given point in time. My local Bahá'í community has changed more in the last ten years than the church of my childhood has changed in the last forty, and the American Bahá'í Community has changed more in the last fifty years than many denominations have changed in the last two hundred. For people who equate tradition with spirituality, clearly the Bahá'í Community is not the way to go. For those who see spirituality as a dynamic, self-directed process, it may very well be.

No one on the planet knows what the Bahá'í community will end up looking like in the future.

Not only is the Bahá'í Community a work in progress, but we are the ones wielding the hammers and paint brushes. The simple fact is that no one—and I mean NO ONE on the planet knows what it will end up looking like. Shoghi Effendi himself said, *"All we can reasonably venture to attempt is to strive to obtain a glimpse of the first streaks of the promised Dawn that must, in the fullness of time, chase away the gloom that has encircled humanity."* This sentence places us seven steps away from actual daylight—that is, an understanding of what the Bahá'í Faith will look like in the future. As far as I'm concerned, that means that your vision is as good as anyone's.

community dynamics

What do I mean when I say the community is constantly changing? If the beliefs and the basic structure stay the same, then what changes? What changes is the concrete application of principles, and the balance between competing goals.

Every organized group of people—from a single family to the United Nations—has to struggle with finding the proper balance between a host of seemingly contradictory needs. Religious communities are no different. In the past, it has been tempting for people to stake out positions in favor of one need over another; to say that one is good and the other is bad, or that one is more important than the other. As humanity has matured, however, it has become more tolerant of the middle ground. The Bahá'í Faith, founded on the principles of progressive revelation and unity in diversity, is firmly committed to the concept of moderation in all things. This does not mean, however, that all Bahá'ís agree on the definition of moderation! Consequently, Bahá'í communities, even more than most, are constantly exploring the benefits of competing needs and goals. If/when you join the Bahá'í Community, you can have a voice in this process. That is why I want to give you a glimpse of some of the issues being discussed in the Community right now.

If you are an American, then you already know that in the U.S. there is a constant balancing process between States' rights and Federal rights, between Congress and the Courts, between rights and responsibilities, between security and freedom, improving services and decreasing taxes, between censorship and public decency, and so on.

In a different way, these same issues and many more have an impact on the personality and spirit of local and national Bahá'í communities. Where is the balance between decentralization and national standards? Should we focus on obeying laws or creating a spirit of forgiveness? Should money be spent locally or nationally, on outreach work or community development, on children or adults? Perhaps most difficult is to balance individual initiative and unified action controlled by institutions.

Here are some of the issues that have changed the shape of the Bahá'í Community since I have been a member. Take a look. Do you have a perspective to offer?

1) The Bahá'í Faith includes social teachings and spiritual teachings. In the last thirty years, the overall spirit of the Community has shifted from being a social activist organization towards being a devotional community. During the 1980's, for example, the community focused a lot on peace. In the 90's it was race unity. In the 00's it shifted towards prayer, devotions and interfaith activities. This major refocus has created an identity crisis of sorts for some individuals and communities.

2) The Faith strongly supports independent investigation of the Truth, but some people are still in need of leaders and "father figures." This is a natural vestige of our maturing process. As the community matures, we can see a shift from individual leaders of the Faith to a focus on institutions. How much do we discourage "hero worship" of members of both sets of institutions? How do we show respect for others without surrendering or denying our own perspectives?

3) Size has a great influence on the spirit of a community. How do we gain the benefits of the resources of a large community without losing the intimacy and connection of a small community? The size of your local community is probably the single largest factor in determining its personality. How can you increase the size if it is small, and how can you increase the intimacy if it is large?

4) The Faith is an independent religion. How does it maintain a distinctive identity while not appearing *so* different that mainstream Americans reject us? We are not "just another church," but we are not a strange and dangerous cult either.

5) Bahá'ís don't take sides in partisan political battles, but we do believe in some very controversial social principles. When does stating your beliefs become political?

6) Education of children is a very important Bahá'í principle, and yet the number of children in any particular community at any particular time fluctuates greatly. How do we meet our obligations in this area?

7) How do we utilize the arts? Should we allow one style of art to be dominant? In the early days in America, for example, one composer wrote almost all of the Bahá'í "hymns." In the sixties and early seventies, folk music and the success of the band Seals and Crofts had a strong influence on the spirit of the Community. During the disco era, Bahá'í music almost disappeared, but with the rise of digital recording, the community is once again flooded with folk, gospel and church-choir music. Which of these, if any, should dominate? How do we help educate people to be more receptive to diverse styles?

8) How do we balance the need to spread the Bahá'í teachings to new areas and the need to maintain critical mass in existing communities? Every few decades, the focus has shifted from expansion to consolidation and back again. Where is the balance?

9) Every social organization, whether political or religious, has to wrestle with the balance between individual rights and freedoms and the needs of the group to limit or control certain types of behavior to protect itself or its reputation. Some Assemblies tend to micro-manage the community, while others allow so much individual initiative that there is no coordination, integration or standards maintained at all. How do we release the energy, creativity and enthusiasm of the individual, while channeling it in healthy and productive ways? How do we distinguish between behavior that feels inappropriate or uncomfortable simply because it is new or creative, versus behavior that is simply inappropriate?

10) Closely related to these questions is the balance between frank and open consultation on one side and avoiding criticism that will undermine the authority of Bahá'í Institutions on the other. Some Local Spiritual Assemblies invite community members to share their concerns, offer advice, even criticize decisions and point out mistakes that may harm the community. Other Assemblies fear any level of disagreement or lack of approval. Likewise, some individuals go along with everything their Assembly says without thinking, while others assume that *any* source of authority must be challenged and attacked after every decision. These extremes on the part of both institutions and individuals are, I believe, simply a sign of immaturity. With maturity comes trust, and with trust comes the ability to be honest without malice or defensiveness.

11) It is important that institutions be allowed to consult on personal problems and sensitive issues confidentially, but it is also important that an atmosphere of secrecy or superiority not be created. Where is the balance?

12) How do you harmonize independent investigation with a coordinated educational program? For many years, people would become Bahá'ís, but were left to train themselves in the basic Bahá'í teachings on their own. Now we have an institute process for new members, but its structured approach may not suit the more independent learners or the long-time Bahá'ís.

13) Buildings buildings buildings. Bahá'ís own some of the most beautiful buildings of any religion in the world, but we also have the smallest number of local buildings per capita of any religion. Most communities hold their meetings in individual's homes, but more and more are starting to acquire Bahá'í Centers. Next to size, the decision to buy or rent a permanent meeting place may be the most important determinant of a community's personality and spirit. Understandably, then, it is one of the most hotly debated issues in many communities.

14) Love and Unity. Some communities focus their energies outwards towards bringing new people in. Others try to create the most loving and unified community possible with the people they have. Some believe you can't have one without the other.

So why am I raising all of these complex issues with someone who is not even a Bahá'í? Well, for several reasons. First, my hope is that if you are interested enough in the Bahá'í teachings to read this entire book then you will eventually want to meet some living breathing Bahá'ís. When you do, if the Bahá'í community is not exactly what you expected, then it is important to *me* that you realize that the people you meet are not *The* Bahá'í Community. They are *your local Bahá'í community* as it exists today. You may like them. You may not. In either case, it is helpful to remember that the community is simply a tool in the global workshop. If you have come to believe in progressive revelation, in the maturation of the human race, the common foundation of all religions and the wisdom of Bahá'u'lláh, then this community of fellow-believers will be a very important tool for your personal growth, even if it drives you crazy some times.

Second, I think it is important to realize that every religion is struggling with these issues. The difference is that many resolve their differences by splitting into smaller and smaller denominations. If you don't like the way one church answers these questions, you don't have to educate, communicate or negotiate, you simply walk down the street to the next church. But there is only one Bahá'í Faith. We have to find ways to organize our communities that respect the diversity of needs and understandings we represent.

This brings me to my third reason for sharing these issues with you. Most people think that when there is a difference of opinion between people it must be resolved by either fighting about it or coming to a compromise. Compromise often means finding a single middle point between two extremes and forcing everyone to move to it. But there is another approach, which is to *celebrate* diversity of opinion. While it may be necessary to temper the behavior of the people on the extreme ends of an issue, there is generally lots of middle ground left for a wide range of activities and opinions. This flexible approach requires a great deal of maturity, tolerance and open-mindedness. It requires a community of people who are willing and able to recognize at least five or six of the seventy-one meanings of every word of God.

So ultimately, I must admit, I have an ulterior motive for sharing some of the issues that Bahá'í communities are struggling with. My hope is that the next great wave of people who join the Bahá'í Faith will be people like you — people who are mature, open-minded, and capable of showing love and respect for people and opinions that are different from their own. While much of the world seems to be drifting towards fanaticism, intolerance and rigidity, the Bahá'í Community has the potential to become a haven for loving, mature, independent-thinking people who realize that spirituality is about how much we are willing to love, not who we are willing to judge.

My hope is that you will take the general outline of the Bahá'í teachings that this book offers, and start imagining the kind of Bahá'í Community *you* would like to live in. If you were a Bahá'í, with no one around to tell you how other Bahá'ís had put these elements together, what would you want to do? How would you want to organize your community? What kinds of meetings, with what kind of music, activities or programs would you envision? What kind of space would you hold these activities in? How would people treat each other? How would you imagine the interaction between individuals and institutions to be conducted? In what spirit? Bring us your vision, and the Bahá'í community will be more vibrant and more diverse because of it.

IMPACT OF DIVERSITY

No matter how much the community changes, grows and evolves, one constant that you can always count on is its diversity. You might think that the diversity of the Bahá'í Community was a result of its global reach, but in fact, its global influence is due to its diversity. The diversity of the Bahá'í teachings themselves attracts many types of people—rich and poor, educated and illiterate, urban and rural, modern and traditional. Consequently, each local community *has* to integrate a much wider cross section of humanity than most other religious or secular organizations. This diversity gives the community a strength, vitality and flexibility that would be impossible to attain if we all looked and thought alike.

Diversity gives the community a strength, vitality and flexibility that would be impossible to attain if we all looked and thought alike.

Let's face it. Sociologists tell us that Sunday mornings are the most racially and economically segregated hours of the week. Most people subconsciously choose their churches based on socio-economic factors first, and theology second. Bahá'ís don't have that option. There is only one Bahá'í Faith, and everyone (and I do mean *everyone*) is welcome. This means that in my 30 years as a Bahá'í, living in dozens of different communities, I have *never* lived in a community that did not have racial, economic and educational diversity. In my first community, for example, my best friends and teachers were a bi-racial couple.

Racial diversity is the most visible quality of most local communities, but it is not the only one that has an impact on the quality and spirit of Bahá'í life. I remember in college having lunch in a restaurant with a good friend and wondering why everyone was staring at us. He was a factory worker with a gray crew cut and I looked like a hippy. He looked way too old and conservative to be my friend and yet too young to be my dad, but we were laughing and having a great time. We sincerely enjoyed each other's company.

Another example comes from when I worked in one of the national Bahá'í offices, many of us would go out for dinner together in small groups of diverse, happy people. Because people knew there were a lot of Bahá'ís living in the area, waitresses would often come up to us and ask if we were Bahá'ís. We were diverse, we were laughing out loud, and we weren't drinking alcohol, so we must be!

This unity in diversity did not come about by accident. It took more than nice words to get us here. It took conscious guidance and encouragement from 'Abdu'l-Bahá, Shoghi Effendi and the Universal House of Justice. It was 'Abdu'l-Bahá who gently explained to the Bahá'ís that we couldn't have separate communities for white and black. It was Shoghi Effendi who told us that overcoming racial prejudice was the most challenging issue facing the American Bahá'í Community. It is the Universal House of Justice that has encouraged social and economic development programs to reach all strata of society. Our unity and our diversity are their legacy.

This unity in diversity did not come about by accident. It took more than nice words to get us here.

A YEAR IN THE LIFE

So what is it like to actually be a Bahá'í? If you dress like most people, eat like most people, go to work like most people, have a family like most people, and say a prayer when you think about it, then you already have a good idea of what it is like to be a Bahá'í on a day-to-day basis. We aren't weird. When I talk about the Bahá'í *Community* I'm not talking about a *commune* with people wearing white robes. I'm talking about a bunch of people like yourself who happen to believe that they have the power to make themselves and the world a little bit better. Yes,

> *If you dress like most people, eat like most people, work like most people, have a family like most people, ...then you already have a good idea of what it is like to be a Bahá'í.*

we might try to dress more modestly than what you see on TV, but then I suspect you do too. Some of us lean towards more healthy and even perhaps some vegetarian foods, but very few of us are fanatics. We don't drink alcohol or take recreational drugs. We try to choose jobs that we feel are of service to humanity, and we work extra hard to keep our families unified. But you probably do too.

When we remember to say our prayers, they are generally prayers from the Bahá'í Writings. We especially try to remember to say one specific prayer each day. We also try to practice a few minutes of meditation during the day, saying "God is most glorious" in Arabic 95 times. That may be unusual, but it is not particularly weird.

Every nineteen days, we get together with the other Bahá'ís in our area for a three-part meeting called Feast. The first part is devotional. We read prayers and Bahá'í Writings, sing songs and try to reconnect with God. People usually take turns reading. There is no "leader," though there is usually an individual or committee acting as host. The second part is administrative. It is like a big family meeting where we talk about goals and finances and even problems. Because it is "family business," it is the only part of the regular Bahá'í life that is not open to the general public. There are no great secrets being discussed, it is just nice to be able to be completely candid without worrying about what other people might misconstrue. Here, the chairperson of the Local Spiritual Assembly acts as coordinator, not president. When we are done with that, then we socialize. It is like a big party every nineteen days. Everyone is welcome. The socializing—getting to know and love each other—is considered as important as the first two parts. Loving God is best demonstrated by loving each other.

The reason we get together every nineteen days, by the way, is that we follow the calendar designed by the Báb. It has nineteen months with nineteen days *Bahá'ís follow a calendar designed by the Báb.* each, with four left over. This may seem unusual, but most people are already aware that there is more than one calendar in the world. The four days left over are placed at the beginning of the last month and are a time of gift giving and charity. American Bahá'ís tend to treat it like Christmas, as it comes at the end of February, and people are in a holiday mood.

In addition to Feast days, Bahá'ís celebrate eleven Holy Days. These commemorate some important dates in Bahá'í history and are open to everyone. Some are parties, some are solemn. Perhaps the most unusual part of just living a Bahá'í life for a year is the Fast that I mentioned earlier. During the last month of the year we don't eat or drink during daylight hours. It is a time of purification and self-discipline similar to Lent.

So this is the universal Bahá'í experience. It would be the same no matter where you lived or when. But it doesn't begin to describe all of the secondary community activities that make each community dynamically unique. It also ignores the sense of

urgency and purpose that drives most individuals within the Bahá'í Community to exert their utmost efforts towards the goal of an "ever advancing civilization."

In any given week, a Bahá'í might attend a devotional meeting, a study class, an informal meeting for people investigating the Bahá'í Faith, called a "Fireside," a "proclamation" event related to race unity or some other social principle, a service project, a conference, a convention, a regional school or a youth workshop, and attend or teach a children's class. All of these activities are geared towards improving one's character, teaching other people about the Faith, or spreading the social principles in an effort to make the world a better place. For members of Bahá'í Institutions, the list is even longer.

All of these activities are geared towards improving one's character, teaching other people about the Faith, or spreading the social principles in an effort to make the world a better place.

a fun place to GROW

If all of this sounds like a lot of work, it is, but it is also a lot of fun—and I think that that is the most surprising thing about Bahá'í community life. When guests attend our parties and pot lucks, they often comment on how relaxed and fun-loving we are; how we can sing and dance together in groups of all ages and backgrounds—without having to get drunk first. In general, I can say that most Bahá'í communities are fun places full of loving people from lots of different backgrounds who are committed to getting along. "Improving one's character" is not about pain and sacrifice, it is about learning how to be happy, loving, and kind. I personally consider the Bahá'í Community my family and can't imagine facing the crazy world we live in without their support.

Perhaps this is a good place to point out the peace and confidence that come from having a positive vision of the future.

If I haven't already mentioned it, perhaps this is a good place to point out the peace and confidence that come from having a positive vision of the future. Bahá'ís are not oblivious to the dangers of a world gone mad. Quite the contrary, Bahá'u'lláh warned us that the world would continue to decline towards immorality and chaos until it was forced to turn towards God. But we see the big picture. We know that the rebellion and pain of adolescence always gives way to the stability of maturity. Always. As a Community we work very hard to make the world a better place. We feel urgency, but we are not frantic. We are not desperate. We do not shake our fists at the sky in frustration. We know that progress is inevitable. Peace is inevitable.

This perspective allows us to be happy and serene without being glassy-eyed and brainwashed. It allows us to work hard without burning ourselves out. It allows us to work together without getting angry and blaming each other when things don't turn out the way we would like right away. And perhaps most important, it allows us to welcome change, growth and maturation without being afraid to let go of the past.

My grandchildren will inherit a better world than the one I was born into—not because of some miracle falling from the sky, but because of the efforts of people like you and me and my Bahá'í friends as we work in harmony with the Will of God to build the Kingdom of God right here on earth with our own hands.

We are working in harmony with the Will of God to build the Kingdom of God right here on earth with our own hands.

from my Bahá'í faith to your Bahá'í faith

Perhaps somewhere during the course of reading this book, you have had an *"Ah-hah"* moment of your own in which things started to make sense to you. Take a moment and consider your feelings. Whether through a flash of insight or a slow process of illumination, have things become clearer since you started reading this book? Are you beginning to understand that God's love for you, your love for God, your spiritual growth, the progress of human kind, the station of Christ, the teachings of Moses, the spirituality of Buddha, the entire history of religion and the entire destiny of the human race all fit into a beautiful, organic, evolving web of life that leaves no one out and welcomes every soul's participation?

Even if you have only caught a glimmer of the possibility that all this might be true, I congratulate you—and welcome you —to a path that will eventually lead you from *My* Bahá'í Faith to *Your* Bahá'í Faith. It is an exciting road.

BIBLIOGRAPHY

Books to help you find out more.

Since Bahá'ís believe in independent investigation of the truth, we
have lots and lots of books that you can use to explore the
Bahá'í Faith on your own. Now that you have read some of the
writings of both Bahá'u'lláh and 'Abdu'l-Bahá for yourself, you
may already have an idea of whether you would rather read Their
words directly, or read books *about* the Faith—either histories or
commentaries like this one.

Though Bahá'u'lláh wrote hundreds of books and letters, only a few
have been translated into English so far. Since 'Abdu'l-Bahá
traveled in the West and corresponded with American Bahá'ís,
there are a few more of his books translated into English.
Shoghi Effendi and the Universal House of Justice provide
additional authoritative works in English. Here are a few titles
you might look for.

Writings of Bahá'u'lláh

The writings of Bahá'u'lláh, as I explained at the beginning of this
book, are full of metaphor, depth, and power. Some people are
ready to just dive into them, while others can meditate on a
single sentence for days at a time and feel spiritually nourished.
If you are a "dive in" kind of person, this is where to start. If
you want to ease in gradually, then consider starting with
'Abdu'l-Bahá, a compilation, or a commentary.

Gleanings from the Writings of Bahá'u'lláh: This is a broad selection
of Bahá'u'lláh's writings, compiled and translated by Shoghi
Effendi. It is one of my all-time favorite Bahá'í books because it
provides very substantive quotations on a wide range of subjects,
organized into five major areas, including God's Messengers and
the nature of the soul.

The Kitabi-Iqan—The Book of Certitude: This is a book-length letter
explaining religious history, progressive revelation and the
relationship between the Prophets.

The Seven Valleys: If your taste runs towards mystical poetry, then
you will appreciate this book. It is a fairly short book that uses
the metaphor of a series of valleys to describe the spiritual
journey towards God.

The Hidden Words of Bahá'u'lláh: You may have noticed several quotations in this book that start with "O Son of Spirit," or something similar. These came from the Hidden Words. It contains about a hundred and fifty short meditations like these. Together, they are said to contain the essence of all revealed truth, so if you only read one Bahá'í book, this would be it. I find them incredibly moving and inspiring. If this were the only book that Bahá'u'lláh wrote, I believe it would be enough to confirm my faith. Since it is a short book, most Bahá'ís keep a few extras around to give away. Ask someone for one.

Books by 'Abdu'l-Bahá

Books by 'Abdu'l-Bahá fall into three categories: books he wrote, collections of letters he wrote, and transcripts of talks he gave. His talks, by their very nature, are the easiest to understand, because they usually address a specific topic within the space of page or two. His letters, however, are so full of love and encouragement that I just love reading them, and his books offer such a depth of insight on a well-developed topic that they are also very enlightening.

Paris Talks: This is a collection of talks that 'Abdu'l-Bahá gave in Paris. It is a fairly short collection, yet it offers a comprehensive and easy-to-read overview of the Bahá'í teachings.

Some Answered Questions: These are 'Abdu'l-Bahá's answers to questions asked over dinner by a Western Bahá'í visiting the Holy Land. Imagine yourself sitting at the table of someone who actually knew the answers to all of life's most persistent questions. What would you ask? Laura Barney asked about life after death, the soul, evolution, the Trinity, virgin birth, free will, the return of Christ, prophecies, and dozens of other interesting spiritual and metaphysical questions. These are some of the most direct explanations of the more esoteric Bahá'í teachings you will find.

Selections from the Writings of 'Abdu'l-Bahá: These are personal letters from 'Abdu'l-Bahá to Bahá'ís in America. While other books make me think hard, this book makes me feel deeply. It makes me *want* to be the kind of person that 'Abdu'l-Bahá invites me to be. It also offers some practical responses to specific questions posed by western correspondents.

MY BAHÁ'Í FAITH

Compilations

Compilations are sometimes easier to follow than straight sacred texts
because they group quotations by topic or in a sequence. Just
remember that compilations reflect the subconscious assump-
tions of the compiler. Having said that, I have found a few
collections that are so well arranged that they have really inspired
me. Since these books are compiled by individuals, they are not
necessarily available on-line, but may be purchased in book-form.

Bahá'í Prayers: There are actually several dozen books with some
variation of this title. Some are expensive; some are designed to
be given away. All of them will offer a selection of prayers by
Bahá'u'lláh and 'Abdu'l-Bahá on a variety of topics, including
health, family, virtues, protection, material assistance and more.

The Divine Art of Living: One of the first and best compilations
designed as a kind of gift-book, with lots of quotations about
God, spiritual growth and social issues. This is a book you can
enjoy even if you have no intention of exploring the Bahá'í Faith
any further.

The Proofs of Bahá'u'lláh's Mission

This compilation begins with writings on the importance of seeking
Truth for oneself, then explains the nature of God's Messengers
and offers several tools for recognizing them.

Bahá'u'lláh's Teachings on Spiritual Reality

This compilation includes writings on spiritual growth, service, God,
the nature of the soul, immortality and many practical as well as
metaphysical questions.

Histories

The Bahá'í Faith: A Short History — Peter Smith: From its roots in
19th Century Persia to its current status as the second most
widespread of the world's independent religions, this book
provides a broad overview.

Bahá'u'lláh: King of Glory; 'Abdu'l-Bahá: Centre of the Covenant;
The Báb: Herald of the Day of Days — H.M. Balyuzi: These
three books provide a fairly extensive and scholarly history of the
Central Figures of the Bahá'í Faith.

Day of Glory (Bahá'u'lláh); Servant of Glory ('Abdu'l-Bahá); Hour of
Dawn (The Báb) — Mary Perkins: These three books offer an
easier-to-read story-based approach to the lives of the Central
Figures.

Introductions and Commentaries:
The Bahá'í Faith: A Short Introduction — Momen: Starting with the
individual, this well-written book explains the influence the
Bahá'í teachings have on the world today.
Gardeners of God — Gouvion and Jouvion: Written by two French
journalists who are not Bahá'í, it offers an outside perspective on
the Bahá'í Community.
The Challenge of Bahá'u'lláh — Matthews: This book takes a
scientific approach to studying the life, teachings and prophecies
of Bahá'u'lláh to determine the validity of His claim.
He Cometh With Clouds — Matthews: An excellent exploration of
the spiritual meanings of the prophecies concerning the return of
Christ.
Thief in the Night — Sears: The most popular exploration of
Christian Prophecies that point to Bahá'u'lláh, it includes both
spiritual prophecies and a surprising number of prophecies that
appear to have been fulfilled literally.
Falling Into Grace, the Trials and Triumphs of Becoming a Bahá'í —
St Rain: When you are ready to take the big step, this book will
offer an honest look at the joys and challenges of joining one of
the world's fastest growing spiritual communities. It is written
by the same author as this book.
Why Me? A Spiritual Guide to Growing Through Tests —St Rain
Also by Justice St Rain, this book offers a compassionate, yet
challenging perspective on using difficulties as tools for acquiring
spiritual virtues.

Where to Get Them:
Some of these books may be in your local library, and many more are
available by special order through any local bookstore, but your
easiest path is to ask a local Bahá'í to loan you some, or to order
them directly from the distributors.
Most of these books plus many more may be purchased on-line from
the publisher and distributor of this book at
www.interfaithresources.com. 1-800-326-1197
Sacred Texts and many additional titles are available from the official
Bahá'í Distribution Service at 1-800-999-9019.
All of the Sacred Texts and many of the secondary works are also
available on-line for free at http://bahai-library.com or can be
downloaded along with an excellent search engine from
http://www.bahai-education.org/ocean/

Justice Saint Rain ✷

a declaration of faith

In signing this card, I declare my belief in Bahá'u'lláh, the Promised One of God. I also recognize the Báb, His Fore-runner, and 'Abdu'l-Bahá, the Center of His Covenant. I request enrollment in the Bahá'í Community with the under-standing that Bahá'u'lláh has established sacred principles, laws, and institutions which I must obey.

Signature _____ Date _____

_____
Full Name – please do not use nicknames

_____
Home address – include apartment or space number

_____
Mailing Address (if different)

_____
City   ST   ZIP

(   )   M / F   / /
Home Phone   Gender   Birth Date

After signing, please tear this page out and give it to a Bahá'í
—or mail it to:
BAHÁ'Í NATIONAL CENTER WILMETTE, IL 60091

Confirmation of Enrollment

To be completed by enrolling institution.

Locality where individual lives: _____

And its Bahá'í Locality Code (if known): _____

Enrolling Agency: NSA, LSA, CBC, ABM

_____ Date:_____
Signature of Authorized Representative

Comments: _____

_____

MY BAHÁ'Í FAITH

If youR next step involves finding out moRe:

If this book has sparked your curiosity but not answered all of your questions, then there are several places to go from here. You can explore the books listed in the bibliography, or you can contact your local Bahá'í Community and start asking questions. To find them you can start by looking in your white pages under Bahá'í. If there is no listing, you can do a search on the web for Baha'i plus the name of your city or state. If that doesn't work, you can call our national contact number at **1-800-22-UNITE**. You can also learn more at our national web site at **www.bahai.net** and our international site **www.bahai.org**. If all else fails, you can write us at **Bahá'í National Center, Wilmette, IL 60091**.

when you aRe Ready to call this home...

By the time you've finished this entire book, you actually know a lot more about Bahá'u'lláh and His teachings than I did when I joined. But what your head knows is not nearly as important as what your heart feels. When your heart tells you that Bahá'u'lláh is the Messenger of God for this age, then you are already a Bahá'í. But in order to participate in Bahá'í Community life, vote in Bahá'í elections, give to the Bahá'í Fund and receive local and national newsletters, you have to tell *us* what your heart has already told *you*. When you sign the simple declaration of faith on the back of this page, including your address and identifying information, you begin a process that allows the Local and/or National Spiritual Assembly to enroll you as an official member of the Bahá'í Faith.